FULL ORCHESTRA

BOOKS BY FRANK HOWES

APPRECIATION OF MUSIC W.E.A.   (Longmans)

BEETHOVEN   Mus. Pilgrim Series   O.U.P.

BORDERLAND OF MUSIC AND
              PSYCHOLOGY   Routledge

BYRD   Masters of Music Series   Routledge

DRAMATIC WORKS OF VAUGHAN
      WILLIAMS   Mus. Pilgrim Series   O.U.P.

KEY TO THE ART OF MUSIC   Blackie

KEY TO OPERA   Blackie

LATER WORKS OF VAUGHAN WILLIAMS
               Mus. Pil. Series   O.U.P.

FULL
ORCHESTRA

FRANK HOWES

LONDON
SECKER & WARBURG
1942

MARTIN SECKER AND WARBURG LTD.

22 ESSEX STREET   W.C. 2

First Published	*April*	1942
Second Impression	*July*	1942
Second Edition (revised)	*November*	1942
Reprinted	*June*	1943
Third Edition	*November*	1943

THIS BOOK IS PRODUCED IN
COMPLETE CONFORMITY WITH THE
AUTHORIZED ECONOMY STANDARDS

MADE AND PRINTED
BY THE WESSEX PRESS
AT TAUNTON IN GREAT BRITAIN

CONTENTS

CHAPTER   PAGE

Preface vi

Preface to Second Edition vii

I. Past and Present 1

II. Evolution 13

III. Tone 28

IV. Instruments Severally Considered 37

§ 1. *Wood Wind*   1. Flute   37

                       2. Oboe   40

                       3. Clarinet   44

                       4. Saxophone   46

                       5. Bassoon   47

§ 2. *Brass*   1. Horn   49

                       2. Trumpet   52

                       3. Cornet   54

                       4. Trombone   55

                       5. Tuba   56

§ 3. *Percussion*   1. Timpani   58

                       2. Drums   61

                       3. The Battery   62

§ 4. *Strings*   1. Harp   65

                       2. Violin Family   67

V. Symphonic Form.. 72

VI. The Symphony 91

VII. Concertos 118

VIII. Dance, Theatre and Programme Music .. 137

IX. Conducting and Conductors 148

Appendix I 164

Appendix II 166

Index 167

Qld St. James's Hall, *by kind permission of the Royal Philharmonic Society.*

The Illustration of *Queen's Hall, London,* in 1922, taken during a Promenade Concert by a staff photographer of *The Times,* shews Sir Henry Wood conducting.

PREFACE

THIS book is designed as a guide to the symphony orchestra and its repertory for the musically inclined reader, the regular concert-goer, the gramophone enthusiast, and the wireless listener. It is, I fear, almost as factual as a text-book, which may make it useful to the student, but it is not, I hope, so didactic as to deter any casual reader captivated by this modern siren, whose song now reaches the big public. Not all of it will appeal equally to all readers. The first part is historical, the middle is technical and the last four chapters are critical. This criticism is based on some seventeen years of assiduous concert-going as a professional newspaper critic. The instructional matter I would defend on the ground that even brute fact is not without interest and, indeed, is necessary as a foundation for the exercise of opinion and speculation. History, I am sure, is essential for the appreciation of style and the formation of taste.

Anyone who writes about the orchestra finds himself deeply in debt to Cecil Forsyth's *Orchestration*. I have also consulted Adam Carse's *The Orchestra in the Eighteenth Century* and *Musical Wind Instruments*, Gorden Jacob's *Orchestral Technique*, and, of course, the relevant articles in Grove's *Dictionary of Music and Musicians*. To these and many another authority, consulted *currente calamo* but not now specifically remembered, I tender thanks. I have also to thank my friend, Mr J. A. Westrup, for reading through my manuscript and checking me up on those thousand and one details that one thinks one knows but afterwards finds one has got wrong. I do not however hold him responsible if any such errors have slipped through; I merely acknowledge in general terms those from which he has already saved me. To my wife I owe a similar debt for pre-

serving me from the worst consequences of my deficiencies as
proof reader as well as for providing me with a touchstone of
judgment on many a musical or literary point.

To Mr. Keith Douglas and the Royal Philharmonic Society
I owe the picture of the old St. James's Hall; to my paper, *The
Times*, the photograph of Queen's Hall, now twice as precious
as when the book was being written; and to my friend, Mrs.
Beatrice MacDermott, the imaginative design on the cover. To
all these I hereby express my thanks.

F. H.

NEWBRIDGE
    JANUARY, 1942.

NOTE:—Musical nomenclature always presents problems of consistency. I have been guided by common usage rather than rigid logic.
Thus I write Monteverde's *Orfeo* but Gluck's *Orpheus* rather than
Orphée, yet Gluck's *Alceste* rather than *Alcestis*, which to the English
reader is not an opera but a play by Euripides.

Similarly I prefer *Casse-noisette* to Nut-cracker for Tchaikovsky's
suite, even though I adopt an English title for the *Sleeping Princess*
ballet and, with some hesitation, the French *Lac des Cygnes* rather than
the uncouth English of *Swan Lake*.

PREFACE TO SECOND EDITION

FRIENDLY critics and critical friends have called my attention to sundry
points requiring amendment. Exigencies of space unfortunately prevent me making any extensive alterations in the text. I am constrained
therefore to make my additions fore and aft: on larger matters here in
these notes and on points of detail in Appendix II.

My chief sins of omission have been occasioned mostly by problems of
classification. Berlioz's *Romeo and Juliet*, which I failed to mention at
all by assigning only one symphony to Berlioz (p.92), is after all described
by the composer himself as a 'dramatic symphony with choruses'.
Similarly the *Symphonie funèbre et triomphale* is a composition for
military band, strings and chorus and was planned for out-door performance. *Harold in Italy* (cf. p.71) ought perhaps to have found a mention
among concertos for viola on pp.133–4, since it is the most extended
work in existence for that instrument, or it might have been included
among the geographical music on p.142, since it contains several Italian
landscapes in its four movements. *Romeo* survives in extracts, of which

the *Scène d'Amour* and the Queen Mab Scherzo certainly have that magic which Berlioz knew how to extract from Shakespeare.

For the same reason, that what I am discussing in a book of this scope is the symphony proper, I have not recognised as symphonies Vaughan Williams's *A Sea Symphony* or Holst's Choral Symphony, although their movements are laid out in the character and order of symphonic movements, because their structure is choral and is chiefly determined by words. Ought I then logically to have excluded THE Choral Symphony? Logically perhaps, but I am not logical—merely reasonable.

On Schubert's Unfinished Symphony I take the view, based purely on the internal evidence of the music, that it was not completed because it was found even by Schubert himself to be too lyrical to be really symphonic. A rose smells as sweet by any other name and the 'Unfinished' is certainly sweet, so that I incur the charge of pedantry in denying it the name of symphony and of dishonesty in suppressing the fact that a scherzo exists in a fairly complete piano sketch and a page of full score. But one cannot say everything in a book of this size. The reasons for its unfinished state may be purely accidental, but to my mind the two existing movements do not go together satisfactorily, as I have indicated in the text (pp.89 and 105).

I was a little severe on modern concertos, (p.131) and with more generosity (and space) might have mentioned among the English composers of piano concertos Donald Tovey, John Ireland and Arthur Bliss, who reasserts the claims of virtuosity in no half-hearted fashion, if only to avoid leaving the impression that the piano is completely neglected by composers of the English renaissance. Having mentioned Walton's violin concerto because it was new, I ought to have made some allusion to Delius's and Bloch's, which are not quite so new but have in their time aroused enthusiasm in the circles of those composers' respective admirers. I can now take the opportunity of alluding to Dyson's and Moeran's violin concertos, which are even newer, but are less inclined to concentrate on the claims of virtuosity. The number of durable violin concertos is not large and this recent manifestation of interest in the form is welcome.

My remarks on drums and their tunings (p.60) could be considerably expanded. In scores before Beethoven, tunings of the timpani in tonic and subdominant are found—for example in *The Creation*, and in certain keys, G and A for instance, the larger drum can take the tonic instead of the dominant. Then again extensions of the compass are not infrequent: even in Schubert's Unfinished Symphony, which only requires two drums, the higher drum plays high F sharp. A special small drum is called for in some modern scores, notably that of *Le Sacre du Printemps*. Notes below E are sometimes demanded by composers. I am told that the soft roll I have mentioned in the 'Romanza' Variation of *Enigma* is sometimes played with two pennies and I have also seen it executed with the finger-nails. Another Elgar *locus classicus* for drums is *Falstaff*, in which the score specifies besides three timpani and bass-drum, a tamburo piccolo, a tambourine and a tabor, the last for pastoral use in Mr. Justice Shallow's orchard in Gloucestershire.

August 1942.

Photograph taken during a Promenade Concert at QUEEN'S HALL, LONDON.   Copyright *The Times*

OLD ST. JAMES'S HALL

(*By kind permission of the Royal Philharmonic Society*)

CHAPTER I

PAST AND PRESENT

ENGLISHMEN have never cared for music as they care for football or film stars. They like singing, most of them, both making a noise themselves or listening to others. There is a long tradition both of religion and conviviality by which men and women who would not claim to be musical will gladly take part in a hymn or join in a chorus. There has been a tradition centuries old by which choral singing in parts has been a fairly widespread pastime. In Elizabethan times it was something more : for about forty years it appears to have been a fashionable craze among cultivated people, and, though it is easy to overestimate the excellence of their performance, the singers of those days conferred an incalculable benefit upon the art of music and a rich heritage upon English musical life by their assiduous practice, thereby stimulating to activity a whole school of first rate composers. Assuredly England has never been a 'land without music', as the reproachful German phrase went a couple of generations ago. But music, musical affairs, musical politics, new compositions, the status of individual artists, has never in this country been "front page news" : the bulk of the population does not really care how music gets along provided that on occasion it can obtain what it wants for ceremonial occasions, for occasional polite entertainment, for lubricating the wheels on which its theatrical or restaurant entertainment runs. In Germany they discuss the migrations of singers from one municipal opera house to another as transfers of professional footballers are discussed here. To us Cup Ties are national events ; our festivals, our opera seasons, and the performance of our virtuosi, even our musical competitions, leave our national phlegm unmoved. The tantrums of a prima donna have a certain human interest for our popular newspapers, but by and large the great public does not care. Are we then a musical people ?

The question is otiose. Are we a blue-eyed people ? Some of us are blue-eyed, and some of us are musical. The musical enthusiasts are a small minority, but the potentially musical are a much larger number. Perhaps five per cent are definitely insusceptible to music—the composer, Holst, whose exceptional experience as a teacher put him in a peculiarly favourable position for examining a cross-section of the community, put it lower at two per cent. The rest are capable of having their interest, and perhaps ultimately their love, aroused for the art. There are many things in this beautiful world that compete for our attention, for our limited time, for our not unlimited mental energy, and for our pocket-money, and many will sacrifice music to geology or bridge or fly-fishing or watching birds or playing billiards or reading poetry. We have only a limited amount of sensibility, and many a gifted person with artistic abilities that run in several directions at once will devote himself to water colours instead of the piano. But the coming of wireless broadcasting has at least made numbers of people, running into hundreds of thousands, aware of music as a factor in their experience of life.

The kind of satisfaction that comes from music—and the nature of that satisfaction is a large philosophical question of the very greatest interest, but not one to turn us off at this early stage of our particular subject—is one of the things that give value to life. Possibly it is the most perfect example of those higher disinterested values that give significance to life, in that it is unmixed with social, political and ethical purposes and so provides us with an instance of what is valuable in and for itself alone without further object. Not everyone will want this particular kind of satisfaction from music; some—most Frenchmen for instance—take a more hedonistic view of it and value it as just one more ingredient in the good life, like the art of cooking only less materialistic in its texture. Still others are content with the opiate of light music. But whichever of the many sorts of psychological satisfaction that can be got from music may be found by any individual, it is so far a part of his life's experience, and more and more people are coming to be aware of it as such and to value it as an enrichment of their lives.

Conspicuous among the musical results of this extension of the franchise by wireless has been the emergence of the orchestra as a predominant candidate for public favour. The conductor has even displaced the prima donna as the proper centre of the spot-light of public regard. The fashion in concerts has changed from oratorio to symphony. Even the fastidious few who are devoted to chamber music feel the seductions of the more potent, the more variously coloured ensemble of the orchestra. I am speaking of conditions in England, and of the changes in English taste since the beginning of the twentieth century. On the continent the opera has always been a rival of the orchestra for musical pre-eminence ; in Vienna on the whole the orchestra had it, in Italy the vocal art. We have had orchestral music in England since Haydn came over to fill an engagement with the impresario Salomon—and even before that, but the present wave of enthusiasm for the orchestra among all sorts and conditions of musical people marks a quite recent shift in our artistic centre of gravity.

The gramophone has also played a part in making people orchestrally minded. Not only can famous orchestras be assembled in the home and told to play what the listener wants to hear, but in the comfort of the domestic armchair Vienna may be compared with New York, Boston and Berlin with the B.B.C. And not only orchestras with their varying tone qualities, but conductors with their different readings of established classics. The veriest ignoramus by diligent listening may learn his Beethoven Symphonies inside out, and put himself into the position of passing an intelligent and comparative criticism upon the different interpretations of Weingartner and Toscanini.

Another factor inclining the public taste towards the orchestra has been the recent great improvement in orchestral playing brought about by a combination of circumstances peculiar to London. London is not England, but it is the hub of England's musical machine. What happened at Queen's Hall made itself felt first at the great provincial festivals, Leeds, Norwich, the Three Choirs, then at all the large towns which are visited by English and foreign orchestras on tour, and finally, through the net-work of local effort which needs professional reinforcement, in the decentralised activities of amateurs. London feeds the provinces. Now, soon after the War, the first German war, orchestral playing was slipshod owing to the prevalence of the deputy system. There is a story told of some foreign conductor who came to conquer England, engaging one of our famous orchestras and paying for several additional rehearsals. He was a little disturbed to notice at his second rehearsal that a horn player who had taken peculiar pains to meet the conduc-

tor's wishes in the phrasing of some important passages was not
present.   At the next rehearsal perturbation deepened to alarm
as he saw so many new faces before him.   More than half of
the orchestra, it appeared, had sent deputies, and the conductor found that it was the custom of the country which he was
powerless to alter for a particular concert.   He felt, however,
that he might be thankful for small mercies in that his principal
double-bass player had remained faithful and he made a point
of thanking the man personally when the last rehearsal was
over.   He was taken aback to receive the answer " That's all
right, sir, but I shan't be coming to the concert".   This laxity
made itself felt in a general slackness of execution, but it encouraged great nimbleness of mind in the individual player who
had to play his part unrehearsed.   Our instrumentalists developed the faculty of sight-reading to a high degree of efficiency, and the cleverer they became the more casual their
attitude to the music.   The British public, grown accustomed
to this easy-going style of performance, was electrified when it
heard the disciplined precision of the Berlin Philharmonic
Orchestra when it first came over here in December 1927.
This apparently was how an orchestra could, and therefore,
ought to sound.   A few quotations from the *Times* notice of one
of its early concerts here (November 1928) give some idea of
the quality of its performance and by implication some indication of what had hitherto been lacking in our own orchestras'
playing.

" The Berlin orchestra's performance is of a kind to which
musicians can listen with pleasure and profit through the most
hackneyed programme.   It is based on a high standard of
finished playing, the essence of which is unanimity in the phrasing. . . Distinctions between *mezzo-piano* and *piano*, and between
mezzo-forte and *forte* were a revelation of control, and there was
pianissimo playing too delicate to be wasted on the first foggy
night of November, which set the audience coughing. . . . .
. . . . . . Every detail stood out with transparent clearness ; the
eight double-basses (few considering the number of the upper
strings) had wonderful resonance. . . . . Nor can we forbear to
mention the drummer, who if he possessed an iron hand kept it
always in a velvet glove, and who afforded some of the most
exquisite moments in an evening filled with rare experiences."

The impression created by the Berlin Orchestra was very

great and our leading orchestral organization at the time, the London Symphony Orchestra, at once took some steps to put its house in order; it engaged the Dutch conductor, Willem Mengelberg, to come and take on the regular conductorship for a season—a break in its traditional policy. This was in the Autumn of 1930 at the very moment when the B.B.C. got together an orchestra and appointed Adrian Boult as musical director in order that he should train the new instrument. The B.B.C. had been giving symphony concerts in London before this, but had now decided on having a more than usually large and complete orchestra of its own, numbering at full strength 119 players, and Boult's first three concerts with it in the autumn of 1930 were a landmark not only in his personal career but in London's orchestral history.

Two years later Sir Thomas Beecham entered the field with a brand new combination, the London Philharmonic Orchestra. It was new not merely as an organization, but in personnel. There had been in London some half a dozen different orchestras, but many of the same players turned up in them all, and their faces were familiar to each other and to the concert-goer. It is said that on the morning of the first rehearsal of the L.P.O. the players eyed each other curiously like a lot of new boys at school. Sir Thomas had picked his instrumentalists here, there and everywhere. He had a number of men just out of their studentship, so that the average age was younger, and their outlook on music not yet hardened. And most of them had never met before. This may be an exaggerated account of what happened, but the new orchestra made a profound impression at its first brilliant concert for the Royal Philharmonic Society on October 7th, 1932.

The London Symphony Orchestra was still pursuing its useful career, so that from 1932 to the outbreak of the second German war there were three first-class symphony orchestras functioning in London, and their differing characteristics have been a source of much discussion, which has in itself sharpened the interest in all things orchestral.

This same period however saw the demise of an orchestra which had served London faithfully from 1895, when it was formed by Sir Henry Wood with Mr. Robert Newman as its manager. It had originally been called the Queen's Hall Orchestra and had been assembled to play at the Promenade

Concerts (hereinafter called the Proms) and its activities were
soon (January 1897) extended to Saturday and Sunday afternoon
concerts in the winter and spring seasons.   It acquired the pre-
fix ' New' when the financial responsibility was transferred in
1915 from Mr. Newman to Messrs. Chappell, the Lessees of
Queen's Hall.   When in 1927 Chappells announced their decision to discontinue their support, the concerts of the New
Queen's Hall Orchestra came to an end.   Throughout its
career the New Queen's Hall Orchestra was associated with
Sir Henry Wood, and thus enjoyed the advantage of a permanent conductor.   Only in the first two seasons had it a
regular connexion with another conductor—the Sunday concerts were conducted by Alberto Randegger.

The London Symphony Orchestra is an offshoot of the old
Queen's Hall Orchestra.   A dispute arose in 1904 between
players and management about the right to send deputies.   A
large number seceded and founded the L.S.O. as a limited company on a co-operative basis—*i.e.* the orchestra became its own
employer.   Its first concert (June 9th, 1904) was conducted by
Hans Richter, but the policy adopted was to commission different conductors for the various concerts.   In the first season
Nikisch, Steinbach, Colonne, Elgar, George Henschel, men of
different traditions, outlook and nationality, played upon the
new instrument, whose adaptability and responsiveness were
noted as prominent characteristics and so they have remained to
this day.   The L.S.O. now nearing its fortieth year, is the
oldest orchestral organization in London, though it is still young
compared to the Hallé Orchestra of Manchester (founded 1857)
and junior to the Scottish Orchestra (founded 1891) and
the Bournemouth Municipal Orchestra (founded 1893).   Apart
from its own concerts in London and its co-operation with
other concert-giving bodies it has served the provinces well by
tours and festival performances.   In 1912 it toured U.S.A.
with Nikisch at its head and it played at the Leeds Triennial
Festival.   Later began a happy association with the annual
Three Choirs Festivals.   Its leader was W. H. Reed, who has
since been honoured with a Lambeth doctorate in recognition of
his great services to the three West Country Cathedrals.   Reed
was a close personal friend of Sir Edward Elgar, and though by
this time Elgar's productive period was at an end, the festivals
of the Three Choirs became in the most natural way festivals of

Elgar's music with the composer directing his own works and establishing a tradition of their performance. The association of England's greatest orchestral composer with this great orchestra is therefore of some historical importance.

The facts just set out serve to confirm the ear's judgement that orchestras have a corporate personality like a boat-race crew or a football team. Continuity of history may even have some bearing on the style of playing. Connoisseurs of today may be able to detect, even behind the dazzling façade of the conductor's personality, something of the corporate life of the orchestras to which he listens either in the hall or on the gramophone record. Actual quality of tone, especially in the wind departments, depends largely on individual instrumentalists, yet when the balance is made up, orchestras offer to the ear of the listener their own peculiar sonority. It has for instance been noticeable during the last years of the decade of the nineteen thirties that the three London orchestras have each a distinctive quality, as well as a general attitude to music, which affects their style of playing. It may be metaphorically described in terms of drapery : the L.S.O. sells a cotton textile, the L.P.O. a silk and the B.B.C. a velvet. Their specific virtues are : of the L.S.O. adaptability and resource, of the L.P.O. a lyric, singing style, derived directly from its conductor's musical mentality, and great finesse ; of the B.B.C. massive power and executive brilliance both corporately and individually. Their compensating defects are : of the L.S.O. a certain colourlessness which sometimes degenerates into laxity (of attack, ensemble and phrasing) ; of the L.P.O. an acuity of tone and attack that sometimes hurts the ear with its assaults—the strings might be whipcord lashes ; of the B.B.C. an inflation that sometimes sounds heavy, sometimes bloated.

The adaptability of the L.S.O. commended its players to Fritz Busch when he took in hand the organization of the Glyndebourne Opera. Busch has very definite ideas about Mozart, about operatic accompaniment and about orchestral performance. He found that the chosen players of the L.S.O. enabled him to get precisely the results he wanted. But he appears to have doubted before he came to England whether he would find here at all what he sought, and the story is significant of the unconscionable time a legend takes to die. This eminent German musician apparently still thought of England as *das Land ohne*

Musik and he sent over an assistant to seek, not very hopefully, possible recruits for the Glyndebourne Orchestra. This prospector told of his astonishment on going into Queen's Hall and recognising at once after only a few bars had been played that the London Symphony Orchestra could actually play a symphony of Brahms, and that we had conductors of our own—Sir Hamilton Harty in this instance—who could give an intelligible account of a standard classic—the E minor symphony.

The B.B.C. Orchestra is a fully salaried body, well paid but hard worked, whose services are reserved to the Corporation. Their concert policy is naturally subservient to their wider musical services to the wireless-listening public, and the division into smaller orchestras with different leaders for special sectional purposes is an arrangement required purely for broadcasting. This subservience goes further in that the Corporation's general political obligations to the country may interfere with musical plans. Hence it came about that at the outbreak of war in 1939 the Proms, which Sir Henry Wood had carried on without intermission all through the previous war years in despite of air raids, were abruptly terminated and the Orchestra evacuted to Bristol, there to dispense such music as there was room for in a curtailed programme and restricted choice of wave-length.

The London Philharmonic Orchestra's financial basis was less secure and the circumstances of war compelled it to reform as a co-operative company like the L.S.O. Trade Union regulations are strictly enforced by the Musicians' Union and the orchestra was soon faced with the alternative of drawing no fees at all as some one else's employee or becoming its own employer. Sir Thomas Beecham had made great efforts to secure sufficient guarantee as a backing for the orchestra he had created, but the difficulties had become insuperable and the formation of the orchestra into a limited liability company was the only, as it was the right, solution of them. The financial problems of keeping a full symphony orchestra in being are great and even a municipality like Bournemouth, which had followed a more or less consistent policy for many years and had derived great benefit, not to say a measure of its material prosperity, from its music, saw fit to reduce its orchestra so cruelly as to mutilate its efficiency. These business details are worth mentioning because they affect the actual constitution and government of an orchestra and to some extent the discipline and the relationship between players and conductor.

The previous history of orchestral music in London resolves itself mainly into the history of two famous institutions, the Royal Philharmonic Society, founded in 1812, and the Crystal Palace Concerts which ran from 1855 to 1901.

The Philharmonic Society of London was formed by professional musicians to perform orchestral music, and its concerts were descended from those of Salomon, who brought Haydn to England for them in 1791 and 1794. Salomon, who was an excellent violinist, was active in the promotion of the new Society and himself led the orchestra at its first concert on March 8th, 1813. Other original members were Charles Neate, who had been a friend and pupil of Beethoven, and who was no doubt partly responsible for the Society's numerous and honourable transactions with Beethoven, at that time the most modern of contemporary composers; Clementi, pianist and composer; Sir Henry Bishop, composer of songs that are still sung; Samuel Webbe, Vincent Novello and William Horsley, all composers esteemed in their day who have left some mark on English music. The musical policy of the new society was progressive and for a considerable time it provided the chief channel for the introduction of new works from abroad and new artists of international repute. As other organizations from time to time appeared and this particular function became less pressing this feature of the Philharmonic programmes became less conspicuous, but with the beginning of the English renaissance the 'Phil' did a great work in providing a platform for the British composer. After a century of honourable work it was granted official permission to change its name to the Royal Philharmonic Society in 1913. In its early days chamber music was also included in its concerts, making the programmes enormously long by modern impatient standards. Two symphonies, two overtures and two quartets and vocal music were regular features, together with a concerto or two. The Society was very active in introducing the works of Beethoven as they came out. It bought from him in 1815 for 25 guineas the right of first performance of three overtures (*King Stephen*, *Ruins of Athens*, and *Overture in C*). And in 1827 it sent him £100 to help him in his illness. The connection with Beethoven remains to this day in the invariable appearance of a bust of the composer in front of the platform at every Philharmonic Concert.

Recent history of the Society has been more chequered, though the standard of its concerts has risen along with the improved execution of all orchestral music in this country. In 1927 there was something like a financial crisis in its affairs and there was no impelling indication of work specially needing to be done to suggest a way out. New works, guest artists, British composers, were now common form and the only policy for the Phil to adopt was to give the best possible performances of the widest variety of works. Sir Thomas Beecham, who had been active for the Society during the 1914 war, again came forward not only as conductor but as a revivifying force in its management, the ultimate upshot of which was the establishment of the London Philharmonic Orchestra with the Society's support. The Royal Philharmonic Society and the London Philharmonic Orchestra are independent organizations, but it is more than coincidence that they have a word in common in their titles.

The management of the Society is vested in a committee of professional musicians elected by the members; members are recruited from a larger body of associates; non-musicians are enrolled as fellows (a curious inversion of the ordinary meaning of the words 'associate' and 'fellow'). The Society has two special higher categories of Honorary Members and Gold Medallists. The presentation of its gold medal is an honour reserved to those who have served the art of music, whether as composers or executants, with high distinction.

The Crystal Palace Concerts started from a lowlier origin and with more humble ideals, yet in their great days they did pioneering work in the introduction of new music, and still more in the kind of educational work among ordinary men and women that has since been done by the Proms. The Crystal Palace became the scene of a Saturday pilgrimage for Londoners, where not only the classics but the romantic compositions of Schubert, Schumann, and Mendelssohn received early performance, as well as those of their successors, like Raff and Rubinstein, who were great in their day but have now dropped out of the canon. This was all new music at the time when the concerts were founded in 1855. Even Schubert was new in the sense that it was left to Sir George Grove, that versatile Englishman, not only to introduce to this country such of his works as were known on the continent in the middle of the century, but to discover more of them in Vienna himself.[1]

The maker of the Crystal Palace Concerts was August Manns, a German bandmaster (1825–1907), who was appointed to conduct the military band that played every day as part of the attractions of a place of popular resort. But his ambitions were for better things and he soon instituted Saturday orchestral concerts, which he directed till they came to an end in 1901. Grove, of Dictionary fame and first Director of the Royal College of Music, was a great power on the committee, and was largely responsible no doubt for the go-ahead nature of the programmes. Even before the English renaissance began with Mackenzie, Parry and Stanford, English works by Sterndale Bennett, Julius Benedict and Arthur Sullivan were performed by Manns. Another feature of these concerts which had a lasting and far-reaching effect was the regular issue of annotated analytical programmes, most of them written by Grove himself.

Just before the end of the Crystal Palace Concerts their spiritual successors were born in Central London, the Promenade Concerts managed by Robert Newman and conducted by Henry J. Wood. The ultimate ancestry of these concerts is to be found in the musical entertainments given in the gardens at Vauxhall, Ranelagh and Marylebone in the eighteenth century. Later series have been organized from time to time at various London theatres but the opening of Queen's Hall in 1893 suggested a new experiment to Newman, its manager, and in 1895 the first season of nightly Proms was given for ten weeks in August, September and October. The season was slightly shortened in 1926 and there was a moment when it looked as though the enterprise might be abandoned, whereupon the B.B.C. stepped in and shouldered the burden which Messrs. Chappell no longer felt able to carry. Eight-week seasons were given until 1939 when the outbreak of war cut Sir Henry Wood's forty-fifth season short. They are still flourishing.

The character of the concerts has become widely known since they were broadcast, the atmosphere of eager enthusiasm and insatiable curiosity finding its way through the microphone to

---

[1] Grove and Sullivan together visited Vienna in 1867 and unearthed the parts of the *Rosamunde* music and generally helped to bring order into Schubert studies.

the distant places of the earth. In the hall, of course, the listener is caught up into a great body of devotees. The assignment of particular nights to particular composers, notably Monday to Wagner and Friday to Beethoven, led almost without the audience perceiving it to a valuable way of listening to music, namely the gradual survey of a composer's output. Comparative study would be an exaggerated description of what the omnivorous audience of the Proms does with its heterogeneous musical experience, but anything like regular attendance soon begins to put order into the listener's knowledge of the orchestral repertory. It is hardly too much to say that the most valuable aspect of Sir Henry Wood's work, especially with the increasing tendency to substitute one-composer for miscellaneous programmes, has been the opportunity it gives to a season-ticket holder to learn the repertory of big works and to be able in the course of a single season to sort out Bach's six Brandenburg concertos, Beethoven's nine symphonies, and Brahms's complete orchestral output, and to make a working acquaintance with the various styles of orchestral composers from Haydn to Stravinsky. The sheer quantity and variety of musical pabulum provided is also a great advantage in that the beginner can take a plunge and find his bearings for himself in a way that is out of the question when he has to choose concerts from sundry series of less frequency. Every critic, professional and amateur, cuts his teeth on Sir Henry Wood, who has been the teacher of an uncountable host of grateful listeners—none the less grateful if perhaps they ultimately outgrow his interpretations.

CHAPTER II

EVOLUTION

THE late H. A. L. Fisher, towards the end of a long life chiefly devoted to its study, declared that he could see no pattern in history. He did not go so far as to say that political history taught no lessons, but he did not believe that it repeated itself, oscillated between two poles, or made any more complicated pattern of events. Musical history, however, is susceptible of a more formal interpretation : it is possible to regard it as in the main an evolutionary process. Certainly both the orchestra and the symphony, the instrument, that is, and the art-form devised for the expression of important musical thought, have shown a continuous state of development for some three and a half centuries. Beyond that we need not go, but taking 1600 as a convenient date-line we see the mediaeval modes of vocal polyphony giving place to keys, simple dance tunes organizing themselves into slightly more complex patterns, these dance forms expanding when key became available as a still wider principle of design, the old suite giving place to the sonata based on key contrast, instruments combining to emphasise the artistic pleasures of balance and contrast, experiments in the combination of instruments gradually issuing in a certain basic tone-plan, the symphony and the orchestra which was to play it emerging in the time of Haydn in the form in which we now know them. Later developments can similarly be traced in an evolutionary plan through the nineteenth century. The modern orchestra playing a symphony represents the highest point evolved in our art. And this highly evolved art has been reached on the soundest Darwinian principles of selection—one cannot perhaps say natural selection—and survival of the fittest. It is the most highly evolved, but not necessarily the greatest, nor the most profound, nor the purest manifestation of musical art. Some of the most profound thought ever uttered in music is to be found in Beethoven's last string quartets, and purity is a quality to be sought primarily in chamber music. The greatest music, i.e. music on the greatest themes, almost certainly involves voices.

For size and theme are legitimate æsthetic categories : a minia-ture may be perfect, but it is not so great a work of art as a large canvas, because from the nature of the case it deals with subject matter of less weight.   Choral music like Bach's *B minor Mass*, Handel's *Messiah*, Beethoven's *Mass in D*, Brahms's *Requiem*, Verdi's *Requiem Mass*, in all of which the orchestra is joined by solo and choral voices, are concerned with the loftiest and the largest of themes the human mind can compass, and their subject-matter determines their status as major works of art. The orchestra alone, however, does deal with large-scale music ; it, too, is capable of adventure and of flights into the realm of the sublime ; it can execute the most subtle nuances of thought and expression ; it may be independent of any story, drama or pro-gramme and may therefore be regarded as pure.   In fact orchestral music is the most highly evolved music which re-quires for its presentation the most highly evolved instrument— the modern full orchestra.   And it is not too much to claim the orchestra as one of the supreme triumphs of the human mind, comparable to the discovery of the wheel, the arch, electric current and the calculus.

Unlike them however, it is by nature an organism, not a contrivance or a machine, and so complex an organism was not created at a stroke nor born ready made.   It was evolved by trial and error, selection and rejection, in a word by the fitness of its components to survive.   It has grown, too, in size since Haydn stabilized its present skeleton.   It reached maturity in Beethoven's Fifth Symphony, though two horns (making four in all) were yet to be added (as they were in the Ninth Sym-phony) before reaching the standard symphony orchestra as specified, for instance, by Brahms.[1]   Beethoven himself in the Eroica Symphony had added a third horn to Mozart's normal complement of two—the trio of the scherzo shows why—so that though he only asks for two horns in No. 5 he had in fact passed the stage when Mozart's normal orchestra would satisfy him.   Clarinets had come into the orchestra in the time of Mozart who marshalled his maximum forces thus : strings plus two flutes, two oboes, two clarinets, two bassoons, two horns, two trumpets, and two drums.   To this Mozartian orchestra Beethoven in the Fifth Symphony added a family of three trombones, and for the extremes of pitch, top and bottom, a piccolo and a double bassoon (contra-fagotto).   Trombones

[1] *See Appendix II.*

had been used both by Gluck and Mozart in their opera scores
for specially solemn effects. Mozart made no use of them in
his symphonies. It was left to Beethoven to make them part
of the normal requirements of the symphony orchestra. In
the Ninth Symphony he went further and embarked on the
extravagance which Berlioz and Wagner, the two great orchestral architects of the nineteenth century, were to encourage.
He retained such 'extras' as the piccolo and contra-fagotto,
brought up the number of the horns to four, and requisitioned
from the theatre band bass drum and cymbals. His further
demand for a choir and solo vocalists is another story and was
not imitated, except by Mendelssohn in *The Hymn of Praise*
(*Lobgesang*), by Berlioz in his ' Romeo and Juliet,' by Liszt in
his ' Faust ' symphony and by Mahler.

More interesting, however, than the tale of gradual aggrand-
izement in the nineteenth century is the earlier history when
the process of selection was being carried out.

Whatever instruments may have been used in the Middle
Ages—and our present orchestral instruments can generally
trace their ancestry to the sackbuts, psalteries, shawms, and
others with equally obsolete names—the point at which combined instrumental music emerges into the open is Monteverde's
opera, *Orfeo*, (1607). Prefaced to the vocal score is a list of
instruments and scattered through the opera are indications as
to which instruments are from time to time to be engaged, but
there is nothing like a modern full score in which the part
assigned to each player is set out on a separate staff, so that the
conductor can see, as well as hear, everything that is going on
at once. It is in fact like the modern condensed score used by
the conductor of a theatre band. Monteverde prescribes about
forty instruments set out in a curiously jumbled order as follows:

Duoi Gravicembani	Two harpsichords
Duoi contrabassi de Viola	Two double basses
Dieci Viole de brazzo	A consort of ten strings
Un Arpa doppia	A double (*i.e.* chromatic) harp.
Duoi Violini piccoli alla Francese	Two piccolo violins
Duoi Chitaroni	Two lutes
Duoi Organi di legno	Two chamber organs

Tre Bassi da gamba	Three bass viols
Quattro Tromboni	Four trombones.
Un Regale	One reed organ.
Duoi Cornetti	Two cornetts.
Un Flautino alla vigesima seconda	One piccolo
Un Clarino con tre Trombe sordine	One first trumpet with three muted trumpets.

This list needs interpretation. The string department contains members both of the viol and violin family. The violino
piccolo is obsolete, but Bach wrote a part for it in the first
Brandenburg Concerto a hundred years later. The organo di
legno was a soft sweet-toned instrument with stopped diapason
pipes ; the regal was a sort of harmonium of much rougher tone,
but capable of crescendo by air pressure from the handblown
bellows. The cornett of the sixteenth century was not the
brass instrument that bears that name today. The two instruments are distinguished by their spelling, but they are alike in
both having a cup mouthpiece. The ancient cornett, however,
was made of wood and had seven finger holes, whereas the
modern cornet belongs to the trumpet-bugle family, in which
the player has to make his notes with his lips, not with his fingers,
and it is provided with valves. The *flautino* (of which actually
two are required in the opera) was of the straight not the transverse kind—a recorder, in fact. The harpsichords were required here for the purpose they served for the next two centuries—to supply chords in accompaniment of the reciting voice.
Viols and violins have a common ancestry from which they
evolved into their final perfection within a year or two of each
other in the sixteenth century. At first the viols enjoyed the
greater favour and were found specially suitable for the domestic chamber music that was fashionable in Italy and in contemporary Elizabethan England. Their tone is sweeter than that
of the violin, which ultimately superseded the viol because its
greater brilliance and power were found more telling as music
came out of the home into public performance. The viol has
a flat back, sloping shoulders and more strings than a violin.
It is held on the knee with finger board uppermost. It
is therefore a leg (gamba) as opposed to an arm (brazzo)
instrument, which is held the other way up with the tail under

the chin. Both instruments were used concurrently for a century, but "les vingt-quatre violons du Roi" in France and the practice of Purcell, following Restoration (*i.e.* French) fashion in England, mark the supremacy of the violin, which was clinched in Italy by the great school of violin writers that was founded about the same time by Corelli. Thus the first operations of natural selection determined that the violin and not the viol family should be the foundation of the orchestra. The last of the viols to survive was the violone or contra-bass viol, which left its mark on the construction of the double-bass for a century after the rest of the viols had become obsolete. Bach writes for it, to provide the fundamental bass to the violin family, in the Brandenburg Concertos.

These Brandenburg Concertos are a landmark in the evolution of the orchestra because they show it before the distinction between chamber and orchestral music had become defined, and they show the process of selection in actual operation, since not all of Bach's instruments survived—familiar instruments of today are found collaborating with instruments that immediately after became obsolete, such as the violino piccolo, already mentioned, in No. 1 and two recorder flutes in No. 4. The oboe d'amore, the oboe da caccia, the viola d'amore and the lute, used in other scores of Bach, also dropped out of use in the next generation. The viols, which have a soft golden tone that is in itself enchanting to the ear, did not survive the seventeenth century in spite of their suitability for chamber music, the reason probably being that the bowing technique of the violin enlarged the possibilities of phrasing. It is not merely on the doubtful issue of tone that the viol was defeated, but on its more limited powers of shapely and expressive phrasing. The violin proved the better instrument for musical purposes and survived.

Another elimination that was going on during this same early stage was that of the plucked string tone, but it took longer to complete, and the harpsichord at least was used after Bach's day not only for the accompaniment of recitative, but as a base of operations for the conductor. When Haydn came to London at Salomon's invitation he directed his symphonies from the harpsichord, but after the end of the eighteenth century harpsichords were no longer built and the conductor emerged as the director of the orchestra. So that in Beethoven's scores we find no provision for plucked string tone and if it is required the violins have to provide it by pizzicato playing. To remedy the deficiency the great romantics, Berlioz and Wagner, introduced that arch-romantic instrument, the harp. But what are one or two harps among their huge forces as compared with the balance of plucked strings against bowed strings in Monteverde, who incidentally forgot to put in his prefatory list the two cithers he prescribes elsewhere in the actual score ? Lutes, cithers, harpsichords, and a harp—the modern orchestra has no sound to compare with this. We may conjecture that the cause of the extinction of this whole class of tonal quality was its weakness. Just as the viol went under, in a contest of stridency, so the weak tone of the lute caused its early disappearance, sped on perhaps by its sheer tiresomeness as an instrument which would hardly remain in tune for many minutes together. The harpsichord survived longest because in combination with strings it lends a distinctive sparkle to the total effect, but the evanescent tone of all plucked strings was swallowed up in the sustained masses of bowed strings and steady wind.

The following instruments, other than the strings, for which Bach wrote in one or other of the Brandenburg Concertos or the orchestral suites, survived and consolidated their position in the orchestra of the eighteenth century : the transverse flute, two oboes, which were often used by Handel to give an edge to violin tone and doubled the violin parts, trumpets which Bach often used in a grouping of three, and the bassoon which he used to support his *basso continuo*. Horns are found in Bach's scores, but his corno was the *Waldhorn* or natural horn and a distinction is made between it and the *corno di caccia* or hunting horn, also prescribed in some of his scores, which was a more ceremonial instrument and less mellow in tone. The horn, that is, was a feature of Bach's orchestra but is a borderline case in our evolutionary computation. It established itself, however, in the third quarter of the eighteenth century and is a constant feature of the scores of Stamitz, C. P. E. Bach, J. C. Bach and early Haydn. It survived because it helped symphonic music through a transitional period of acute change.

Between J. S. Bach who died in 1750 and the mature work of Haydn, which for convenience we may put as beginning in 1780, instrumental music underwent a radical change of style and the orchestra underwent a similar transformation. We may observe at work here the evolutionary principle of adapta-

tion. In these thirty years the principle of design known as
sonata form emerged from a long process of gradual development. It has proved an enormously fruitful principle, æsthe-
tically satisfying, and bringing to instrumental music unaccompanied by words enormously increased powers of extended
levitation—sheer length, in fact, and sustained flight without
endangering the feeling of unity. Bach's instrumental works,
when they are not suites of dance forms, are constructed on the
principle of the Ritornello, a recurrent main theme from which
all the material of the movement is derived. These movements,
which are to be found in his concertos, may therefore be described as unitary (or monothematic). In scoring them Bach
paid no attention to the individual peculiarities of the instruments—they all played the same tune in turn and somehow
contrived to execute the same figuration—trumpets had to be
as agile as violins and oboes often doubled string parts. Furthermore he orchestrated them on a plan which has been
compared to an organist's ' registration ' (or choice of stops),
though the good organist nowadays is careful to avoid this
particular way of laying on his colour : he assigned a particular
instrument or group of instruments to a particular movement,
and indeed relied on the consistency of instrumental colour so
obtained to help in characterizing the movement. The oboe
d'amore, it might be, would thread a strand of counterpoint
through the polyphonic texture, if not continually, at any rate
consistently, from beginning to end of a movement (or vocal
number) : it was distinctive and obligatory and was hence
called *obbligato*. The next movement would have an obbligato
of a different instrument—a violin, maybe, or a horn. The score
of the *B minor Mass* shows very well how the system worked.
An opening ritornello stated the material of which the particular
number was to be composed : it consisted of a strongly featured
melodic line for the obbligato instrument and an accompanying
texture of strings, each pursuing a line of its own over the basso
continuo played by violoncello, violone and bassoon. Across
this polyphonic texture chords were thrown by the harpsichord
which served to bind the counterpoint into a harmony—for
Bach's counterpoint is conditioned more than Palestrina's or
Byrd's by considerations of key and harmonic progression.
The harpsichord player made up his part as he went along on
the basis of the figures written beneath the bass which indicated

in shorthand the chords required to fit the counterpoint. He
' filled in ' in fact any spaces that might occur between the high
melodic line and the deep bass continuo.

This method of scoring became completely outmoded in the
course of the quarter century between Bach and Haydn. Horns
and oboes are capable of sustaining harmony between treble
and bass even better than the harpsichord, and it only needed
to brighten their tones with flutes and to mellow it with clarinets to have at the composer's disposal a chorus of wind
instruments, which he could use, not in the manner of an
obbligato, but all together either with or without the strings to
sustain the harmony, to reinforce the tone and to exploit the newly
discovered powers of tonal gradation by crescendo and diminuendo. These changes in the way of handling an orchestra are
associated very largely with the name of Johann Stamitz and
the orchestra which he conducted from 1742 to 1757 at the court
of the Elector of Mannheim. The concurrent changes in the
music which brought about the changes in the orchestra are
chiefly attributable to Bach's son, Carl Philip Emanuel (1714–
1788). We hear very little of either of these two men's works,
or of Emanuel Bach's brother, Johann Christian, who was also
writing symphonies in the new style at the same time. When
we do we are apt to find them dull, because Haydn and Mozart
did the same sort of thing much better. The result is that
we have very little knowledge of the years 1740-1780, when
one of the greatest changes in music was being effected, and find
it difficult to come by the knowledge of what exactly Stamitz
and the Bach sons did for music.

In particular it is difficult to ascertain what went on at Mannheim. The histories and biographies are fond of referring to
" the famous Mannheim School " and leaving the reader in
ignorance of what that fame precisely consisted in.

Joseph Stamitz (1717–1757) was a Bohemian who made a
reputation as a violinist. In 1745 he was appointed as leading
violin and director of the Elector's chamber music. The line
between chamber and orchestral music remained indeter-
minate till the middle of Haydn's career. Stamitz was also a
copious composer but his niche in history is secured for him by
his orchestral discoveries and reforms. He began, being a
string player himself, to emancipate the violas by giving them
something more interesting to do than repeat the bass an octave

higher, though complete emancipation did not come till later in the century. The idea of using the wind as a chorus may have come to him from the serenades he wrote for outdoor performance where a harpsichord was not available. Gluck a little later was to oust the harpsichord from the orchestral pit of the theatre, though he continued to write obbligato parts for solo wind instruments, as in the familiar ballet music from *Orpheus* with its prominent use of the flute. Stamitz at some time towards the end of his life admitted the clarinet, invented half a century before, into the orchestra. We know that the Mannheim Orchestra boasted two clarinets in 1758 but that was a year after Stamitz *père* (he had two gifted sons who carried on the good work of developing symphonic form and symphonic orchestration) had died. Clarinets, we know, were used in Stamitz's symphonies when they were played in Paris five years previously in 1753, but his scores do not specify parts for them and the practice at the time was for them either to double, or to deputize for, the oboes. Mozart heard them in the Mannheim Orchestra much later in 1778 and wrote full of enthusiasm for the new instrument to his father; he was moved to include them in the " Paris " Symphony which he composed in that year for the Concert Spirituel. Incidentally Mozart speaks slightingly of Stamitz's symphonies by calling them ' noisy '. The noise however had made Stamitz famous : like Rossini he invented a special crescendo effect. It attracted all the more attention because up to his time the main dynamic interest in music had been a blunt antithesis of loud and soft, often little better than a mechanical echo effect. By means of crescendo and diminuendo Stamitz opened the way to the vast possibilities of gradation of tone.

The position, then, as the eighteenth century entered on its last quarter is that natural selection has eliminated all the instruments which are not fit to survive in the orchestra as it now prepares to undertake the work of operatic accompaniment and symphonic performance. Strings are there as the foundation ; trumpets and drums are there for their special purposes which they have discharged for centuries ; certain wind instruments have established themselves, notably flutes, oboes, bassoons and horns. The new symphonic style is to show almost at once how these various groups are to co-operate and make an agreeable blend of tone. Mozart never actually standardized the wind band at two apiece of flutes, oboes, clarinets, bassoons, horns and trumpets, though that is a composite picture of the Mozartian orchestra. Even as late as Beethoven's Fourth Symphony one finds a single flute sufficing. Mozart's practice is worth examination in detail.

Out of fifty-six symphonies and divertimenti, sixteen have as their only wind two oboes and two horns. In fifty-four concertos for various instruments (including thirteen for solo wind) twenty have this same small wind band. In addition this combination of oboes and horns is found in ten symphonies and three concertos with the addition of trumpets and drums. Mozart enriched his orchestra as he grew older and we find about K. 180[1] that the bassoon makes increasingly frequent appearances : we can add to the oboe-horn-trumpet scheme two bassoons in the case of four more symphonies and two concertos. There is a greater variety in the scoring of the concertos than in the symphonies because the solo instrument, whatever it is, disturbs the ordinary symphonic lay-out in tone colour. Thus flutes are only found in eleven of the fifty-seven symphonies (including as always divertimenti) while the concertos show seventeen flute parts. The sequence of thirteen piano concertos from K. 450 onwards have (all but one) a single flute, the usual oboes and horns and two bassoons ; in two instances only are two clarinets employed. The four flute concertos are accompanied just by oboes and horns, and there is a certain amount of evidence to show that the obbligato character of the flute tended to linger. It is for instance occasionally found as a solo instrument in a slow movement, and nowhere else in the same work. Even in the last three great symphonies there is only one flute in the score. Mozart uses two flutes in place of oboes in K. 41, K. 114, K. 130, K. 134 and K. 199 (five instances). He uses two flutes in addition to the oboe-horn-trumpet combination in K. 161, in the " Paris " symphony where he also uses a pair of clarinets (K. 297), in K. 318, in the " Prague " Symphony (K. 504) and in the Serenade (K. 320). The general deduction therefore is that Mozart gradually grafted on a treble and a bass to his two medium-voiced wind instruments to form a wind quartet, and flirted with clarinets as opportunity offered.

The clarinets first appear in the Divertimenti (K. 113) of

---

[1] K. stands for the number in Köchel's great catalogue of Mozart's compositions based on chronological order.

1771 but not again, except in Divertimenti and Serenades for Wind (without strings), which are obviously on a different footing, till the "Paris" symphony of 1778 and thereafter only in the late E flat symphony and as an afterthought to the great G minor symphony. The "Jupiter" is without clarinets and has a part for only one flute. But the clarinet is a little commoner in the concertos. It has for instance to take the place of the oboes, if the solo instrument is an oboe (as in K. 293). Three piano concertos have parts for two clarinets. When the clarinet is soloist (as in K. 622) the accompaniment is for two flutes, two horns and two bassoons. In the horn concerto (K. 447) there are clarinets instead of oboes. In spite therefore of his enthusiastic praise of clarinets to his father, Mozart did not himself make any great use of them, probably because they were not even by the end of his life very commonly available or were not well enough played. They were however establishing themselves as members of the wind chorus. Even without them the wind chorus could play full harmony, so taking the place of the harpsichord and helping to develop the new symphonic style of writing for orchestra as opposed to the old obbligato style. In Beethoven's First Symphony (1800) the orchestra is for two each of flutes, oboes, clarinets, bassoons, horns, trumpets and drums plus the standard strings. It was not to be stabilized at this strength for long, but there it is with its several departments, strings, wood-wind, brass and percussion, developed to maturity ready for the symphonic developments of the nineteenth century.

Beethoven's own additions to this orchestra, so conveniently dated 1800, we have already chronicled. It is noteworthy by the way that the dates in musical history are for the most part as convenient and memorable as musical terminology is loose and illogical.

By 1824 when Beethoven gave the Ninth Symphony to the world he had increased his demands to four horns and three trombones, as well as wanting a piccolo and a double bassoon to be added to the top and bottom of the wood-wind chorus. The four horns now became standardized. They were required primarily because owing to the nature of the instrument (see Chapter IV) a pair of horns could not physically produce all the notes required by the composer, but if a second pair were added, crooked in a different key (and thus, as will be explained, making available a new series of notes), something like a complete scale became available, though not yet chromatic semitones. This particular problem was to be solved on quite other lines in the middle of the century by the invention of valves. But in music, as in economics, maxima tend to become minima, and four horns became the nineteenth century norm for that department until the later extravagance of Wagner and Strauss began to ask for eight. Schumann, Mendelssohn, Berlioz and Brahms all required two pairs of horns in their symphonies. In concertos two horns may suffice, as they did for Beethoven in the ' Emperor ', but Berlioz (in *Harold in Italy*, which is the equivalent of a viola concerto) and Brahms in all four of his concertos specified four horns. Brahms did however dispense with trombones in the concertos though he required them in all four symphonies.

The actual growth of the wind departments of the orchestra was however determined more by operatic than symphonic practice. It had been so in the eighteenth century—the most conspicuous instance of such a tendency being Gluck's and Mozart's use of trombones in opera before they were used in the concert orchestra. We in England, who have no operatic tradition, are apt to overlook the influence which the theatre has on other branches of music, but it is not difficult to see how that influence comes to be exercised. In the search for greater vividness of dramatic expression composers call in every available, or if it is not available every imaginable, kind of tone colour ; instrument makers turn their wits to the problem of richer tonal resources, and the sober writers of symphonies enter in and take possession of any new territory conquered by the explorers and inventors. And so Berlioz, the writer of programme music, and Wagner who wrote almost nothing outside the theatre, are the master-builders of the nineteenth century orchestra.

The process of selection by trial and error went on after the main wind chorus had been established. Berlioz in his *Treatise upon Instrumentation and Orchestration* devotes sections to a number of instruments that are now obsolete— the keyed bugle, the ophicleide, the bombardon, the serpent, the Russian bassoon. The ophicleide and the serpent are alike not only in their name—for ophis is Greek for snake—but in their methods of sound production and manner of playing, *i.e.*

they belong to the horn family, in which the lips applied to a cupped mouthpiece produce the notes of the harmonic series (see Chapter IV), while intermediate notes are obtained by the use of holes and keys, like those of wood-wind instruments. They are to be found in some scores of Mendelssohn, their function being to provide a bass for the horns, but they were never satisfactory and Berlioz has some pungent commentary on them, comparing the ophicleide to a bull in a drawing-room and describing the serpent as essentially barbarous, fit rather for use in sanguinary religious rites than in the services of the Church. Their extinction was assured when the invention of valves improved the horns and provided a satisfactory bass for the brass chorus in the bass tuba.

Berlioz was, like another French composer, Debussy, interested in sonority for its own sake, and not merely as clothing for thematic ideas. Not all his experiments come off. There is for instance a place in the *Grande Messe des Morts* where he writes high chords for three flutes which are intended to pick up the harmonics of a fundamental[1] sounded on a unison of eight trombones—a sound-image perhaps symbolising the heights and the depths, above and below the voices in prayer, but it merely makes an unconvincing and unbalanced sound.

In his search for increased sonority and new varieties of it Berlioz began by increasing the numbers of the wind chorus and so seeking a new tonal balance. His mind ran to extravagance of every sort and the resources he asked for this Requiem Mass were specified as follows :—Four flutes, two oboes, two cors anglais, four B flat clarinets, six horns in C, six horns in E flat, eight bassoons, twenty-five first violins, twenty-five second violins, twenty violas, twenty violoncellos, and eighteen contra-basses. This band was to accompany a chorus of seventy sopranos and altos, (who mostly sing the same part), sixty tenors and seventy basses. But in addition he prescribes four orchestras of brass (each consisting of four trumpets and four trombones, with the addition in some cases of cornets and tubas), which are to be placed away from the main body of singers and players and disposed at the four quarters of the compass. His requirements of percussion include two big drums, three pairs of cymbals, and a gong besides the generous allowance of sixteen timpani to be played by ten players (though with the im-

For fundamental and partial tones (harmonics) see Chapter III.

proved instruments of today fewer timpanists would suffice).
The additions in this swollen mass requiring note are the cors
anglais and the cornets. The cor anglais is neither English
nor a horn but an alto oboe. Although it is found as early as
Purcell, and Gluck had prescribed it in the scores of *Orpheus* and
Alceste, it was not acclimatized to the normal orchestra until
Berlioz and Wagner regularly demanded it. The oboe family
was not completed till Strauss in *Salome* and Delius in the *Mass
of Life* called for the bass oboe or heckelphone. The tendency
however to complete families of tone, as a modern organ builder
does, began to operate all through the century. The bass
clarinet was introduced by Meyerbeer in *Les Huguenots* and
Le Prophète, and its soft, almost treacly, tone appealed strongly
to Wagner and in his scores contributes to that characteristic
sonority of deep velvet pile which we probably owe to the sensitiveness of his skin. There are high E flat clarinets of a more
piercing quality than the normal instruments in B flat and A
which are brought in for special effects, like the representation
of the spiteful critics in *Ein Heldenleben*, and an alto clarinet,
equivalent to the corno di bassetto for which Mozart wrote
obbligato fashion in *La Clemenza di Tito* and the *Requiem*, is
available. Only the bass clarinet however has become a regular
member of the wind chorus.

The cornets, of which Berlioz constantly asks for a pair to
march with the trumpets, are fairly common in French scores,
but in England the instrument is associated with brass and
military bands rather than with the orchestra. Its tone is less
brilliant than the trumpet, but it blends more readily and is
more flexible in execution. The Germans do not use it nor is it
found in Wagner's scores. Wagner however does demand
eight horns in *The Ring*, of which four are sometimes replaced
by the so-called Wagner tubas, which are really saxhorns (brass
valve instruments of the bugle type) fitted with a mouthpiece
that makes for a soft-toned quality—another instance of Wagner's search for a feather-bed softness of sonority.

The flute added to itself the piccolo, and in some exotic scores
the bass flute, which with an inaccuracy characteristic of musical
terminology is not a bass but an alto flute. Wagner demands
three flutes, exclusive of piccolos, in *The Ring* and Verdi in the
famous consecration scene in *Aida* uses three flutes playing
chords. Actually this use of three flutes to suggest a particular

atmosphere had been anticipated by Bach (notably in an aria about a river—not the Nile—but a river none the less). Holst in *The Planets* wants four flautists, of whom two in some of the numbers of the suite are told off to play piccolo and bass flute, but in "Venus" the atmosphere of unearthly peace is suggested by all four flutes playing chords.

The number of string players was naturally augmented to keep pace with this growth in the number of wind instruments. Wagner's proportions for *The Ring* are fifteen wood-wind, twenty-one brass, harps and percussion, and sixteen each of first and second violins, twelve each of violas and violoncellos and eight double basses, making over a hundred players in all. Strauss in *Ein Heldenleben* requires an equal number, disposed in much the same proportions. Beethoven for the " Eroica " had thirty-five players all told. In less than a century the orchestral population had trebled itself. A Malthusian reform was due in the twentieth century.

CHAPTER III

TONE

THERE are four ways of producing sound :—

(1) The beating of an elastic surface.
(2) Blowing air through suitably organized cavities.
(3) Setting stretched strings in motion.
(4) Creating an electro-magnetic disturbance.

The fourth is a new-comer and though it has been used in the manufacture of musical instruments, notably pipeless organs, it has not yet been employed in the orchestra. The other three sources of sound production have been known and used from time immemorial and they give the ground plan of the orchestra by classifying its instruments into percussion, wind and string groups. The piano, whose position in the orchestra is dubious and occasional, is a hybrid in that it combines the percussion and the string principles, since its strings are beaten with hammers.

The three main categories are subdivided as follows : percussion is of two kinds, consisting of instruments that yield notes of definite musical pitch, like the kettledrums, the glockenspiel, xylophone and celesta, and of instruments that yield only attractive noises, like the bass drum, side-drum, triangle and cymbals. Wind instruments are generally divided into wood and brass, but the brass French horn might almost be considered a member of the wood-wind group because of its mellow tone, leaving the trumpet and trombones with their more strident timbre to constitute, along with the lumbering tuba, the heavy brass division of the orchestra. Flutes, which are often made of metal, head the wood-wind band which consists of oboes, clarinets, and bassoons besides. Here, however, we encounter further sub-classification. All wind instruments consist of tubes in which a column of air vibrates under regulated control, but the vibration may be set up in one of several different ways, and the control exerted by one of several different types of mechanism. You can blow into a hollow tube, and if there is a rim, lip or edge to catch your breath, it will set up the right kind of disturbance in the tube to issue as a musical note—such are flutes, both the straight and the transverse sort (*i.e.* tin and bamboo whistles, the flue-pipes of the organ and recorders on the one hand, fifes, ocarinas, flutes and piccolos on the other). You can alternatively blow into a pipe against an edge that is not firm and fixed but is free itself to vibrate, namely a reed. Reeds may be single as in the clarinet where the reed beats against a mouthpiece and causes vibrations in the tube by rapid closing and opening of the aperture between reed and mouthpiece, or reeds may be double and beat against each other, as in the oboe and bassoon. The brass instruments, inasmuch as they employ the player's lips as a kind of double reed, come into this category, but that is not the whole story, which is complicated by two other factors, shortly to be considered, key mechanism and the harmonic series.

The strings are homogeneous except for the harp which is plucked, whereas the violin family, backbone and mainstay of the whole orchestra, uses bows made sticky with rosin to set the strings in steady periodic motion. It is in the distinction between sustained and plucked string tone that the modern orchestra chiefly differs from its ancient forbears; indeed it is not too much to say that the chief defect of the modern orchestra is the absence of plucked string tone, which gives attack to phrasing and flecks sustained tone with a sparkle. The modern harp is too specialized in timbre to contribute to the general ensemble, whereas a harpsichord as used with violins in the eighteenth century gives a touch of effervescence to the general mass of string tone. Before the lute became obsolete, it was used in large numbers with other instruments, and a satisfactory modern substitute for it, of sufficent power to maintain itself among the gigantic racket of modern orchestral forces, has never been found. When a composer must have the distinctive sound of the plucked string, he instructs his violins to play *pizzicato*. Tchaikovsky writes a whole movement in his fourth symphony during which the string players put their bows down and twang their strings with their fingers. But no device has yet been found for supplying the ingredient which the lute did to the ensembles of the seventeenth century and the harpsichord to the ensembles of the eighteenth. Instead the tendency throughout the nineteenth century was to thicken and enrich orchestral sonority, and subsequent reaction has been on quite other lines, towards what is bare and brittle rather than what is luminous and sparkling.

Musical sound consists of regular periodic vibrations of the air reaching the ear and falling on its drum. This highly sensitive organ translates the vibrations into the sensation which the brain recognises as sound of definite pitch. If the vibrations are neither regular nor periodic, but on the other hand are spasmodic and disorganized, the brain registers the sensation as one of noise having no ascertainable pitch.

Sounds are produced by vibrations which are excited in the various ways described—by blowing, hitting, scraping or plucking elastic membranes of one sort or another. The blowing, hitting, scraping and plucking impart to the sounds a recognisable difference of attack and a varying degree of success in sustaining the sounds, but they do not account for the startling difference in quality, tone-colour or timbre, as it is variously called, which is the most striking difference between the same note played at the same loudness upon (say) a violin, a clarinet, a trumpet, a piano or a human voice. It is this variety of tone colour which is the chief fascination of the orchestra. What is its secret ?

The answer is mathematical. Mathematics and music have a certain basic connexion, which has fascinated, but always in the last resort baffled, theorists who have tried to work it out. The musical ear will not tolerate the systematization of mathematics. Having found out the mathematical basis for correct intonation it throws it overboard and prefers something out of tune. The two most flagrant instances of this aural contumacy are vibrato and equal temperament. But an even earlier rebellion occurs in the harmonic series, which we must now examine, where the ear declares that some of nature's own intervals are out of tune.

If you strike and sustain deep bass C on the piano, what you hear will not be that low C in all its individuality and purity but a rich compound of tones. You will in fact hear the following chord :—

N.B. The notes representing the 7th, 11th, 13th & 14th partials lying to the right of the main chord are approximations to their actual pitches which are 'out of tune.'

The note you struck is called the fundamental and the other tones enclosed in it are called partial tones, because they are present in less strength than the fundamental. They are sometimes called upper partials, sometimes harmonics, and the whole chord is known as the harmonic series. In general the higher you get in the series the weaker the partial. Theoretically the partial tones continue in the mathematical series indefinitely, but acoustically they are negligible above the 24th, and even organ builders, who build artificial partials into the tonal schemes of their instrument in order to secure brilliance of tone in what is otherwise a rather dull and muffled timbre, begin to cheat when they reach the higher notes of the scale. What begin as the seventeenth, nineteenth, and twenty-first harmonics suffer a 'break' about half way up and fall back an octave lower. For theoretical purposes the sixteen notes shown in the harmonic series above are enough to explain the phenomena of tone quality and for practical purposes the higher harmonics soon fade out.

The partials in the series have been numbered from 1 to 16, but we have already begun our jiggerypokery with the mathematics. In order to make the ratios in the series serve our purposes we have called the fundamental its own first partial. This logical anomaly enables us to observe from a glance at the ordinal numbers that the interval of an octave which appears first in the series 𝄞 may be mathematically stated as the ratio 2 : 1, and the interval of a fifth, 𝄢 whose notes are numbered 2 and 3, can be represented as the factor 3 : 2. Thus, if the pitch of bottom C is given by 64 vibrations per second, its octave will be 64×2=128, its double octave $128 \times 2 = 256$ and treble c'' will be 512. Baritone G will be $\frac{128 \times 3}{2} = 192$. Every note then, has its pitch determined by the number of its vibrations per second. Modern acoustics, in penetrating the further mysteries of wireless waves, prefers the term 'cycles'. The old term 'vibration' meant a complete double vibration per second which may be represented graphically thus ⟨‿⟩. The ratios of the intervals of the harmonic series therefore must be understood to be ratios of vibration numbers (or frequencies). Our treble c'' may be said to have a frequency of 512 cycles. Accepting this standard of pitch for convenience, though actually what we hear in our concert halls is a little higher, we can use the harmonic series as a table in which the numbers 1-16 will give us the ratios for the various musical intervals—octave, fifth, fourth, third, tone and semi-tone. To find the ratio representing a major third we look up the series till we come to a major third, which first appears between c' and e', and observe that it may be numerically stated as 4 : 5 and if we are curious to know what the frequency of e' is, knowing that c' is 256 we can multiply by $\frac{5}{4}$ and get 320.

For the most part musicians are not interested in frequencies and prefer to trust their ears for correct intonation. The ratios however have some importance because they correspond to a fact of aural psychology, viz. that the ear regards the higher numbers as progressively discordant. The interval represented by 15 : 16 is a strong discord ; the interval represented by 1 : 2 is so smooth a concord that it is often incorrectly called a unison —it is not a unison, but an octave, but the two sounds so completely merge that the ear is lulled into accepting the two sounds as one sound and the tongue follows suit and calls it a unison, (at any rate for the purpose of congregational singing). In the history of counterpoint the fifth 2 : 3, has always been regarded as a perfect concord. Fourths (3 : 4) though concordant have to be negotiated with care in early counterpoint, while the third (4 : 5) was not regarded as truly concordant and would be avoided, for instance, in a final chord. After the emergence of key as a guiding principle in the seventeenth century the major third came to be regarded as a perfect concord, though the minor third (5 : 6) was still too harsh a discord to be admitted to a final chord, and was replaced in the last cadence by the major third or *tierce de Picardie*. In the eighteenth century the minor third was accepted as concordant and a piece might end on a minor chord. Delius in the early twentieth century ends every one of his *Songs of Farewell* on a chord of the added sixth which contains the interval 12 : 13. So that the ear is a very corruptible organ and can be persuaded to accept much that it once rejected. It cannot however be induced to abandon altogether its mathematical standards of concordance ; the lower the figure of the ratio, the purer the concordance of the interval.

One apparent anomaly in reading the table occurs in the third octave of the series : two different ratios 5 : 6 and 6 : 7 can be obtained for the same interval, the minor third. The smaller figures are correct ; the $g'—b\flat'$ interval is less than a true minor third, and that is why the natural seventh is said to be out of tune. The interval of a tone is represented by the ratio 8 : 9 and the semi-tone by the ratio 15 : 16. The system of tuning known as Equal Temperament causes complications in the ratios of intervals, but the orchestra does not play consistently in the rigid equally tempered tuning of the keyboard instruments so we need not pursue them.

The purpose of this long digression into acoustics may now be disclosed : no explanation of tone colour can be made without reference to the harmonic series, and the mechanism of brass instruments cannot be described without it.

Tone colour (timbre) is due to the presence, selection, and relative strength of partials in what the Germans call a *Klang* i.e. the composite tone sounded by a single note. If a tone has few partials as in a flute, tuning fork or dove's coo, it will be smooth and dull ; if it is rich in partials, it will be rich in quality ; if it is rich in partials of which the upper ones are strong relatively to the lower ones, it will be brilliant, as in a trumpet ; if it is rich in upper partials relatively to the fundamental, it may present the fascinating quality but ambiguous pitch of the church bell.

The first six partials are present in varying degrees of prominence in most instruments. The piano, the open diapason of the organ, the human voice, show these six partials in moderate strength. The tone becomes rough when partials above six are present in moderate strength, and actually brays (as in the *cuivré* or brassed effects of the brass instruments) when they are present above six in great strength. When only the odd numbered partials are prominent, the tone is hollow, as in the

clarinet (which has a strong seventh partial) and certain
stopped organ pipes. If the fundamental is strong, the tone
given by odd partials is rich ; if the fundamental is weak relatively to the upper partials, the tone is poor.

The flute is an open pipe in which all partials are theoretically possible, but only the prime tone and the second partial
are detectable : hence its smooth tone. The oboe and bassoon
contain the ordinary partials up to 16, the intensity of which
decreases regularly as the series ascends ; the oboe owes its
incisive quality to the presence of the partials above six. The
clarinet, as already mentioned, specializes in the odd-numbered
partials. The brass instruments are rich in partials, but the
matter is complicated by the fact that the actual notes played
are formed by the player choosing to reinforce by the vibrations of his lips one or other of the partials in the series given by
his open tube.

This theory of overtones as the determinants of tone colour
was worked out by Helmholz (1821–1894) and has never been
superseded, but it has been refined on. It has been observed
that the shape of an instrument, whether conical or cylindrical,
the shape of its bottom end as cup or bell, and the material of
which it is made, whether of wood or metal, affect the tone of
a wind instrument. The bell and the bore of the instrument
will no doubt produce their effect by their influence on the
partials, but it ought not to make any difference to the vibrating
column of air inside a wind instrument what its walls are made of.
If the sounds were purely air-produced, such differences as
occur in wooden, zinc, tin, and alloy metal of organ pipes could
not arise ; it is the air inside, not the encasing material, whose
vibrations produce the sound. Actually however, the encasing
material does vibrate on a frequency of its own and does in consequence affect the quality of sound. Its own frequencies will
coincide with and reinforce some of the higher frequencies of the
vibrating air column. This property of the instrument, which
is found in violins and the human voice as well as in wind
instruments, is known as a ' formant '.

The term ' formant ' was first applied to the range of vowel
sounds from *oo* to *ee*. It was observed that choirboys singing
the vowel *ee* in a resonant building were heard as singing *oo*
because the high partials which determine the peculiar sound of
ee are evanescent and leave only the lower partials in effective

operation. Helmholz's analysis of vowel quality gave the following dispositions of the partials at the same pitch.

For *oo*   harmonics   1, 2, 3.
"   *oh*   "   1, 2, 3, 4, 5.
"   *ah*   "   1, 2, 3, 4, 5, 6, 7, 8.
"   *eh*   "   1, 2, 3, 4, 5.
"   *ay*   "   1, 2,   6, 7, 8.
"   *ee*   "   5 and others much
                                                     higher.

Sir Richard Paget's more recent investigations confirm and elaborate Helmholz's findings. Since the rule is the higher the weaker, *ee* sounds easily degenerate into *oo*. The shapes of the resonance chambers in the throat and mouth are therefore the formants. But the term is now applied to the properties of instruments, and it is chiefly the formants which account for the difference among violins between a Stradivarius and a seven-and-sixpenny box. The natural vibrations of a violin body are somewhere between three thousand and six thousand. These high frequencies reinforce the higher partials set up by the vibration of the string and give the particular instrument its own distinctive tone, over and above the general quality of string tone which can be explained in terms of the harmonics in the harmonic series. In fact, besides Helmholz's relative pitch theory of timbre we now have to consider an absolute pitch theory of tone quality. Quality in fact is not homogeneous throughout an instrument's range, as it should be if Helmholz's theory was the whole truth of the matter, and the marked differences of colour found in the three registers of the clarinet are unaccountable as coming from one and the same instrument, if the instrument itself had not got its own preferences. These preferences are formants. A silver flute will have one set of free vibrations, a wooden flute of the same dimensions and pitch will have a slightly different set because of the different densities of wood and metal, and the result will be a difference of tone colour.

Formants however are not responsible for the broad distinctions of tone colour, on which the composition of the orchestra is based. They may account for the difference between a broad, an acid and a sweet tone from the oboe, though here no doubt the reed and the player share the responsibility. Handel's oboe and Mr. Leon Goossens's oboe make different kinds of sound, but both are peculiar to the oboe and composers do not specify sweet or acid in their scores, nor do they prescribe whether the flautist shall use a silver or a wooden flute.

With the general principles of classification and of tonal quality in mind, we can proceed to examine in more detail the behaviour of the various instruments comprised in the modern orchestra, glancing at their earlier history as we go. It will be convenient to take them in the order in which they appear in the modern full score, beginning with the wind and taking the percussion out of its evolutionary order—for it is probably reasonable to suppose that primitive man, like his modern representative, the human baby, begins his musical experience with the drum—and considering it after the heavy brass and before the strings. We begin therefore with the flute and piccolo.

CHAPTER IV

THE INSTRUMENTS SEVERALLY CONSIDERED

I. THE WOOD-WIND

THE generic name of the group of breath-driven instruments which top the page of the score and confront the conductor full-face on the platform is the wood-wind. Wood-wind, that is, as opposed to brass-wind. The distinction is more than one of material. Flutes, oboes, clarinets and bassoons *are* made of wood, and horns, trumpets and trombones *are* made of brass, but the two categories are differentiated more by their methods of sound production than by the physical stuff of which they are made, more by the technique of playing than by their marked differences of tonal quality. They serve different orchestral functions. These sharp distinctions will appear as the members of each group are severally described.

THE FLUTE

The transverse flute seems to have obtained its ascendancy over the fipple flute some time in the eighteenth century, since the last appearance of the latter is in Bach's fourth Brandenburg Concerto, and since the transverse flute was long known as the German flute it may very well be that, as Germany led the way in instrumental composition, it was German taste that placed the sideways flute at the top of the score as the high soprano of the orchestra. Both instruments are of immemorial (and there-fore equal) antiquity, and the recorder, a straight-played pipe with a mouthpiece, is having a modern revival as a solo instru-ment, but it is the transverse flute with a mere hole for embou-chure (technical name for the mouthpiece in all wind instru-ments and such variation in its effective size as can be made by the application of the lips to it) that has served for the two centuries of orchestral music. It maintained its solo character longer than the other wood-wind instruments; Mozart was content with one flute but it entered the orchestral chorus as a pair with Beethoven, and it is possible that the keen interest of amateur soloists helped to bring about the improvements in the instrument that were made in the last century. These improvements consisted in reconciling the conflicting claim of acoustics and fingering.

If holes were bored in the tube of a cylindrical pipe at the places where they would give the notes of a diatonic scale in tune, it does not follow that they would lie under the fingers of a normal pair of hands nor that they would be of the precise diameter to fit the pad of the finger-tip. It was found by process of trial and error how the two claims could best be compromised; the optimum length having been thus determined, the other dimensions, bore, diameter of finger holes, placing of embouchure and so on, were adjusted to it so as to yield the most satisfactory tone quality, the greatest possible evenness of tone through the whole range, the most correct intonation and the greatest ease of fingering. The mutual adjustment of all these claims, musical, physiological, mechanical, is the instrument-maker's chief problem. In the case of the concert flute a cylindrical tube nearly two feet long which gives D (beneath the treble stave) as its open note established itself as the best of the available compromises. The player blows a stream of air horizontally across a hole cut about two inches from the stopped end of the tube; vibrations are set up thereby in the tube; the finger holes are a device for acoustically shortening the tube. To sound the lowest note all the holes must be closed. Six finger holes will therefore give one octave of a diatonic scale. A further octave is obtained by overblowing, i.e. blowing harder so that the air column is encouraged to break up fractionally according to the laws of the harmonic series. Thus the player by changing his embouchure (in this case contracting his lips so as to direct a narrower stream of air against the edge of the hole) secures the first harmonic instead of the fundamental note of the pipe, and incidentally increases the admixture of edge tones (a subsidiary series of vibrations that adulterates the tone of the flute) and adds to the difficulty of playing softly. In the third octave he has to call in his fingering to help his embouchure to secure the break-up of the pipe into the smaller fractions required. Still he has no chromatic notes and is therefore restricted in his range of key. Other holes could however be bored and if they lay beyond the reach of the player's available fingers they could be closed with a pad and opened by a lever key. The first key was added to the flute in the seventeenth century, and Quantz, the famous flautist at the Court of Frederick the Great (himself an enthusiastic flautist), says that it was adopted in Germany at the beginning of the eighteenth century. Over a hundred years were to elapse before this method of increasing the resources of the flute was carried to its logical conclusion and a complete chromatic scale provided by the use of a key mechanism which brought every note within easy reach and control of the player's finger. It was in 1832 that Theobald Boehm invented the mechanism of silver rods and felt pads that bears his name and fully enfranchised the instrument so that it has become the most flexible of the woodwind group and can, so to speak, play anything.

It is the lack of overtones that gives the flute its character for good and ill. It is the most neutral of all the instruments in the orchestra and will take on opposite emotional characteristics according to the context. Perhaps the most conspicuous instance of this ambiguity occurs in Bach's *St. Matthew Passion* where in two successive numbers it impartially signifies tenderness and ferocity. In the aria " The Saviour now is dying " a flute obbligato is all compassion ; in the following chorus a screaming top line adds a touch of savagery to the angry shouts of the mob ," Let Him be crucified ". When it is used in the minor mode it may through lack of overtones sound quite ghostly, as in the famous D minor solo which Gluck wrote for Orpheus in the Elysian Fields. In a major mode it stands more chance of picking up some of the faint partials of the harmonic series ; at any rate it is capable on occasion of boldness, especially in its middle and top registers. The defiant, triumphant call of the flute doubling that of the horn in the finale of Brahms's first symphony—the held note followed in descent by a Scotch snap—is the outstanding case of the heroic use of an instrument which in general inclines to sweetness and the feminine virtues.

The piccolo flute, on the other hand, half the size and an octave higher in pitch, has the temperament of a terrier. It is capable of soft playing and decorative use, but its function is brilliance, as in the coda of *Egmont* Overture, where it enhances the headlong rush of the orchestra, and it revels in storms from Gluck's tempest in *Iphigenia in Tauris* to Beethoven's Pastoral Symphony. It is capable of special effects, as in its grotesque association with the bassoon in the drinking song in Weber's

Der Freischütz. The second flautist in an orchestra is expected to play piccolo when required. The piccolo therefore may appear not on the top but on the second line of a full score in spite of the fact that the highest notes of all are assigned to it. Its part is written an octave lower than it sounds.

THE OBOE

The oboe, also a treble instrument, is in all respects unlike the flute. It is a reed instrument with a tone rich in partials, of an incisive character, very definite in its pastoral associations, and, unlike the flute, capable of considerable gradation of tone. Its compass is a little less than the flute's which has a full three octaves from middle C. The oboe can get down by means of a key extension (whose effect is to lengthen the pipe) to B flat, but it will not soar beyond G in alt. Its use in pairs in the wind chorus is to give richness of tone and power of crescendo. In pre-symphonic days oboes often doubled string parts, and Handel used numbers of them in unison as support for voices in his oratorios.

Their history is the story of their refinement, but there is less difference in the use of the instrument from Lully and Purcell to the present day than is shown by any other wind instrument. The crucial date is the end of the seventeenth century when the shawm of the fifteenth and sixteenth centuries turned into the modern oboe. The shawm family had a coarse tone suitable for outdoor use by Waits, Town Bands, and Military Bands. Shawms were provided with six finger holes, which the oboe to-day retains, for the primary diatonic scale of an octave. In the eighteenth century the instrument was made in three pieces and one or two keys were added. In the nineteenth more keys were added to produce the chromatic scale—the oboe followed the example of the flute—and a narrower reed was adopted to give a more delicate tone. The shape of the oboe is slightly conical and it overblows at the octave. The name is found in various forms. The English ' shawm ' is equivalent to German ' schalmey ', French ' chalamie ', and Italian ' piffero '. The name ' bombarde ' was also used in all four languages, suggesting onomatopoeically the buzzing sound of the lower-pitched members of the family. The bassoons also derive from this family and a distinction within this chorus of six double-reed instruments into ' haulx bois ' or high wood, and ' gros bois ' or big wood, as the two large bass bombardes or pommers were called, has given the oboe its modern name. Hautbois is French, hautboy is good English (pronounced o-boy), Italians use oboe, which is also good English (plural : oboes or oboi).

Apart from its use in chorus, the oboe excels as a singer of sustained melodies—the tunes Schubert writes for it as the first subjects of the Andante of the C major Symphony and of the first movement of the Unfinished Symphony, where it is doubled by the clarinet in unison, occur at once to the mind. It may however also be used *staccato* in company with the other reed instruments to make a chatter like that of the Apprentices in *Die Meistersinger* or to be positively spiteful as in the Critics' section of Strauss's *Ein Heldenleben*. Its predominant quality is plaintive and in the hands of modern players like Mr. Leon Goossens, who has added a vibrato to its tone colour, it loses its fundamental acidity and becomes almost sentimental in its sweetness. Incidentally Mr. Goossens's playing, which owes its supreme excellence to the subtlety and control of phrasing, has enlarged the scope of the oboe by elevating it to the ranks of a concert soloist. Even Mozart, who wrote something for most instruments, only left a fragmentary concerto for the oboe, so that it has been left for modern English composers, inspired by a single executive artist, as they have also been inspired by the viola playing of Mr. Lionel Tertis to write extended and important works for the viola, to turn out concertos for the oboe. Mr. Leon Goossens's brother, Eugene, Dr. Gordon Jacob, and Rutland Boughton have successfully dealt with the problem of giving to an instrument, which tends from its very decided and individual tone colour to cloy if continuously used, the opportunity to show its variety in extended concertos.

Other members of the oboe family in current use are, if the Irishism be allowed, the obsolete oboe d'amore prescribed by Bach for obbligati in the Passions and other elaborate Church music; the similarly obsolete oboe da caccia, which was the predecessor of the cor anglais; the cor anglais itself, an alto oboe; and the bass oboe or heckelphone. The oboe d'amore and the cor anglais are what are known as transposing instruments, which means that the notes written for them are instructions to use certain fingerings rather than indications of the sounds to be produced. This arrangement, whereby their parts are written

in a different key from that of the piece in which they are par-
ticipating, is fantastically inconvenient to the reader of the score
but makes life simpler for the player.   An instrument such as
the violin, which plays the notes on the paper, is said to be
" in C ".   The player thinks of the notes in his head, and his
fingers proceed to find them on his instrument.   Certain wind
instruments, however, if built in C are found to have inequali-
ties of tone or to develop other difficulties of execution.   It is
found by experience for instance, that clarinets are more convenient to handle if they are built in B flat or A. The formants
of a particular wind instrument may produce an optimum tone
from a certain length of pipe which does not give C as its open
note, and other technical considerations that make for ease of
playing have brought about the distressing necessity of writing
for them in the wrong key if they are to sound the right notes.
Flutes and oboes are actually built in D, *i.e.* to sound D as their
natural note, but they are not treated as transposing instruments.
The reasons for treating an instrument as a transposer or a non-
transposer are not logical but practical ; it is the convenience of
the player, as discovered by experience, that determines whether
his part shall be an instruction to his fingers or to his ear.   The
oboe d'amore is built and sounds a minor third lower than the
oboe ; it is therefore in A.   The player blows C and it sounds A;
his part therefore is transposed up a minor third.   If then, the
piece is in C major, the part for oboe d'amore (or clarinet in A)
will be written in E flat with three flats in the signature.   Or
think of it this way : A major has three sharps in its signature ;
the player on an instrument built in A therefore starts with a
bias of three degrees of sharpness ; if he is to play in C this bias
must be offset by three degrees of flatness.   To cancel out the
effect of this native sharpness in the instrument the composer
must write with three more flats or three less sharps than his
main key contains.   If his piece is to sound in G major with
one sharp he will write for his transposing instrument in B flat
with two flats.   The system is maddening to everyone but the
player.   The player however can read his oboe d'amore part
straight off with his oboe fingering and produce the right sounds
if this allowance for key shift has been made by the composer.
Similarly the cor anglais is built a perfect fifth below the oboe ;
it is therefore in F ; if middle C is blown baritone F will emerge
from the bell of the instrument ; the composer writes for cor

anglais with one flat less or one sharp more than the key signature of the music. Silly, but it works ; and the conductor who has to read a bunch of these transpositions must make the best job he can of it.

The oboe d'amore has a somewhat milder tone than the oboe, a difference which was probably all the more noticeable in the eighteenth century when Bach used it as accompaniment, either singly or in pairs, for some of his most tender arias. The oboe da caccia, which Bach also employed, has a deeper and more plangent effect, and as used in the *St. Matthew Passion* conveys the extremity of grief in long cantilena passages of thirds and sixths, e.g. in the aria " Ah Golgotha ".

The modern cor anglais similarly conveys melancholy. The opening of the third act of *Tristan* has a long unaccompanied passage for cor anglais which is ostensibly a shepherd's pipe but speaks of the world completely lost, following as it does the heavy harmonies that tell of Tristan's mortal sickness. Berlioz uses the instrument in less unhappy contexts, in the *Carnaval Romain* Overture, for instance, and in the *Scène aux Champs* of the Fantastic Symphony, where it merely sounds pastoral. It has been used in symphonies by Dvorak and Franck, in both cases in the slow movements. Conservative critics regarded its appearance in the symphony orchestra as a proof that Franck's work was no true symphony. This was ridiculous, but it indicates that the cor anglais, even more than the oboe, is an individualist whose place in an ensemble has to be prepared with care. Actually the cor anglais can be used to strengthen the middle harmonies and enrich the texture of the wind chorus. It is used with three oboes and a shrill clarinet by Strauss in the Critics' Section of *Ein Heldenleben* for the special effect of incisive and vigorous malice, but French composers, who are fond of it and first established it as part of the normal forces of the orchestra, regard it as a noble (Berlioz's word for it) and deep-feeling instrument. The heckelphone or bass oboe, called after Heckel its inventor, is not much used. Strauss and Delius have called for it in one or two scores. It is a transposing instrument in that it is written an octave higher than it sounds so that an oboe player can transfer his finger technique to it without change, but as the transposition is an octave it avoids all the tiresome difficulties of key change and occasions no difficulty in score reading.

The Clarinet

By derivation of its name the clarinet ought to be a little trumpet, yet the tone colours of the two instruments in modern times are poles apart. But we have been reminded of the connexion in recent years by Toscanini's deplorable substitution of a clarinet for a trumpet in the second Brandenburg Concerto. Our soft-spoken modern clarinet in B flat or A is not the only possible sort of clarinet and a smaller instrument in E flat is shrill and hard. Even a clarinet in C, which is prescribed by Beethoven in his score of the Ninth Symphony, soon came to be regarded as too hard for the work which the clarinet was called upon to do in the orchestra of the nineteenth century. The building of the instrument in keys demanding transposition is therefore required for the production of the soft-grained, smooth tone that is now regarded as characteristic. Even so the instrument is not homogeneous throughout its compass which is broken into three portions. Of these the lowest register with a dark and hollow tone is called the chalumeau. This is the same word as 'schalmey' or 'shawm', ancestor of the oboe, and it rather looks as though that word was at one time applied generically to any treble reed instrument. For the clarinet has no sort of relationship with the oboe. It uses a single not a double reed, it is cylindrical in shape, though its bell gives it a somewhat tapered appearance, and it overblows, not at the octave like the flute and oboe, but at the twelfth (*i.e* at the third instead of the second harmonic), which terrifically complicates the fingering and is in the last resort the reason why two clarinets are required by the player, one for flat and one for sharp keys.

The invention of the clarinet is usually attributed to a seventeenth century German flute maker, J. C. Denner. It is supposed that he found a single reed chalumeau and, by opening a hole at the right place in its tube, enabled the instrument to be overblown. The function of the hole is to help break up the length of the tube so as to make it yield the higher partials. The hole must be closed for the natural octave (produced by seven finger holes), and for the purpose of opening and shutting this vent-hole Denner invented the speaker-key. The chalumeau had no bell; the clarinet acquired one during the eighteenth century and finger keys were gradually added to complete its compass and make it more playable. It was therefore a new instrument during the early part of the century and only entered the symphony orchestra during Stamitz's reign at Mannheim (see pp. 20 and 93) and was not fully acclimatized even by Mozart. In the nineteenth century the various mechanisms on the lines invented by Boehm for the flute enabled more holes to be bored (and closed by keys) so as to give a complete chromatic compass of three and a half octaves. There is a patch of half an octave in the middle, just above the chalumeau register where the line is weak, but above that it is at once pure and rich. Its power of gradation and sensitive phrasing is very great ; it is flexible, it can trill and shake, and it can skip wide intervals ; staccato notes can be obtained by ' tonguing ', a process employed on all wind instruments whereby the air stream can be cut off short by direct action of the tongue upon the embouchure. The clarinet speaks easily and so little abruptly that its attack may be compared with the gentle strokes of the bow on the strings of the violin ; for this reason it takes the place of the violin in military bands.

Its special character may be better appreciated in chamber music than in the orchestra, since two immortal quintets for clarinet and strings are in the repertory of the instrument, by Mozart and Brahms, both of whom were moved to write for the clarinet by exceptional players, Mozart by Stadler and Brahms by Mühlfeld. Mozart, Weber and Stanford have written concertos for it. The orchestral repertory offers endless examples of striking passages for the instrument. There come to mind : the pianissimo quotation in the thirteenth of Elgar's ' Enigma ' Variations of the phrase of Mendelssohn to signify " Calm Sea and Prosperous Voyage " ; the dark fate theme on the low register in Tchaikovsky's Fifth Symphony ; and the exquisite caress of Brynhilde's Love and Sleep themes in *The Ring*. Wagner certainly had a partiality for the instrument, including the bass clarinet, insomuch as he liked soft, furry, sounds. Wagner indeed provides an interesting example of synæsthesia. He had an abnormally sensitive skin ; he not only required silk underclothes but had his walls hung with satin and was in every nerve sensitive to light. This sensitivity appears in his orchestration with its lush, luxurious sonority. Recent reaction against Wagner fastens on this creamy, oily sound-texture as peculiarly repellent. But if you like it, as the majority of us are bound to like it, even while it chokes us, it is balm to the ear.

Clarinets and horns are the chief ingredients in it—though his harmony, as spelled by divided strings, enhances the impression —and a conspicuous symptom of his peculiar tone-texture is to be found in his use of the bass clarinet.

This is a true bass instrument in B flat. At one time an alto clarinet called the basset horn (corno di bassetto) was in use— Mozart has parts for it in *La Clemenza di Tito*, in *Il Seraglio*, in the *Requiem* and in *Die Zauberflöte umlaut*. Just as the ordinary clarinet is a true soprano but has a range down to baritone D, so this alto (or rather tenor) clarinet has a deep bottom register going as low as bottom F (a bass-baritone's bottom note, F below the bass stave). Its place in modern scores is taken by an alto clarinet in E flat (or F) which is commonly found in military bands, as is another soprano E flat clarinet that sounds an octave higher and whose transposition is a minor third upwards. This last instrument makes an occasional appearance in the orchestra, and Strauss especially inclines to its employment. The bass clarinet has a tone at the opposite pole from this hard-edged high clarinet and is more oleaginous than the ordinary B flat clarinet. Its shape differs from the instruments of medium pitch in that to secure adequate length both the mouth-piece and the bell have to be bent over. Its music is sometimes written in the treble clef with two flats less, or two sharps more, than the main key, and its sounds are then a ninth lower than the written note, or it may be used in the bass clef when it sounds a tone lower than written. To Meyerbeer goes the credit, it would seem, for first exploiting the possibilities of the bass clarinet, as there is an important part for it in *Les Huguenots*. Wagner naturally liked its soft, sombre tones and used it in *Tristan* at the crisis of the second Act as well as in *The Ring*. Tchaikovsky obtained a light-hearted, because grotesque, effect from it in the " Danse de la Fée Dragée " of the *Casse-Noisette Suite*, where it is accompanied, upside down as it were in pitch, by the celesta.

THE SAXOPHONE

Akin to the clarinet, in that they are transposing instruments with a single reed and have a similar, though devitalized, quality of tone, are the members of the saxophone family. The saxophone was invented about 1840 by Adolphe Sax and in 1846 he patented two sets of seven instruments, one for orchestral and one for military use. He could not have foreseen that its chief opportunities would occur in jazz bands. To this day the orchestral employment of the instrument is more frequent in French than in other scores. The two extreme sizes never obtained favour but the others are in common use. They differ from the clarinets in that they are made of brass and have a conical bore (which causes them to overblow not at the twelfth but at the octave). They are therefore hybrids with no evolution behind them. They are used in military bands, especially on the continent, and they are probably the most successful of any instruments that have been devised and launched ready-made and fully grown-up on the art of music. Their tone is at once voluptuous and hard-faced—hence their suitability to the twentieth century dance-hall. They have been used by Vaughan Williams in *Job* to depict hypocrites, but a saxophone plays its part quite innocently when it takes its turn in Ravel's *Bolero*, or says its say in Bizet's *L'Arlésienne*.

THE BASSOON

There remain in the wood-wind group the bassoons. The bassoon is called *fagotto* in Italian and *Fagott* in German, owing no doubt to its resemblance to a faggot, which is a bundle of sticks. For the bassoon is too long a pipe to be playable unless it is bent in half, and its two columns, bound together and fitted with a twig-like projecting mouthpiece, form a rudimentary faggot of maple wood. The French name is *basson* and means just what it says, for the instrument has formed the bass of the reed group since its invention in the sixteenth century. We have Englished its name into bassoon, and our poet Coleridge incorrectly attached the epithet 'loud' to it. It is not a bit loud but a modest double-reed instrument, the bass equivalent of the oboe with a compass of three and a half octaves. It is dryish in tone and if played *staccato* easily sounds grotesque. It has often enough been called the buffoon of the orchestra on the strength of its comic possibilities, but a better title is the gentleman of the orchestra since it is both hardworking and easy-going, and, when it comes to the point, so dignified in tone and so refined in execution as to merit an aristocratic title.

The doubling of the pipe solved two problems; it reduced the gross length to the manageable dimensions of about four feet and it enabled holes to be bored in both parts of the tube so as to be accessible to the player's hands without an excessive amount of rods and key mechanisms. The bend in the pipe is embedded in a single piece of wood and is U-shaped. Into this joint are fitted on the one side the ' wing ' and above that the crook which holds the reed, and on the other the long joint which projects right out and up to the bell.

The musical capacities of the instrument may be observed in Mozart's bassoon concerto. In the time of Bach and Handel it was used to double the violoncello as part of the basso continuo. Beethoven really cared for it, and in addition to making two bassoons a standard component of the wind chorus, took every opportunity of adding decorative solos or counterpoints by the way. Elgar also seems to have had a special affection for the bassoon.

The double bassoon sounds an octave lower and is used as the contra-bass instrument of the wood-wind group. Its sound is like that of the pedal reeds of the organ, very sonorous and telling without being particularly loud. In the $\frac{6}{8}$ variation of the finale of the Choral Symphony Beethoven uses it with bass drum and cymbals to give a kind of celestial snort. The sublime and the ridiculous are very close together in the movement, as close in fact as they are in a gargoyle set among a lapidary communion of saints, and there is always the suggestion of heaven being a glorified circus from this combination of abysmal grunt and clanging cymbal. There is also a part for the double bassoon in the Fifth Symphony and in Brahms's first and third symphonies. Subsequently it became a regular adjunct to the wind department of the orchestra.

II. The Brass

With the brass we come to an entirely different principle of tone production, and the technique of playing horns, trumpets and trombones necessitates an entirely different style of writing for these inside pillars of the orchestral mass.

Any tube, whether cylindrically or conically bored, yields a note corresponding to its length when the air within it is set in periodic vibration. Bugles, trumpets and horns, which from time immemorial have been used for the outdoor music of fighting and hunting, are such open tubes fitted with a suitable mouthpiece, consisting of a rim against which the lips of the player can make an air-tight contact. The player's lips thus form a kind of double-reed and his skill consists in adjusting the tension of this reed till its frequency corresponds with that of the tube. The tube is capable of other frequencies than that of its fundamental length, namely the natural harmonics. But it is only capable of producing one harmonic series, that of its open note, whatever that may be.

THE HORN

Now it will be apparent that a horn player with an instrument whose fundamental is bass C, produced by a pipe sixteen feet long, has not at his disposal a complete scale. In fact until he comes to the third octave of its compass he has not even a triad, and only gets a diatonic scale in the fourth octave. Even so the notes corresponding to the seventh, eleventh, thirteenth and fourteenth partials are not in tune, there is no chromatic note until the fifteenth partial, nor can in fact the player produce his bottom (fundamental) note at all owing to the looseness of lip that it would require. The same considerations apply to the natural trumpet. The player, then, on a natural horn or trumpet was very limited in what he could do. He had, in Cecil Forsyth's words, " eleven healthy and four decrepit notes only " and so could not play much more than a tally-ho or a fanfare. Thus the instrument had to undergo a good deal of development before it could play more than a very limited part in serious music. Salvation was ultimately (i.e. about 1850) found in a system of valves. The method of tone production however remains unaltered ; it is tied to the harmonic series of a particular length of tube and the player chooses the notes he wants from it by varying the tension of his lips so as to pick up the corresponding harmonic.

The first attempt to extend the capacities of the natural brass instruments was to make available for them varying lengths of tube, which would give more than one harmonic series. Arrangements were therefore made to insert in the length of the tube, now neatly coiled into manageable contortions, further coils of tubing which gave various new total lengths and therefore various fundamental notes with their accompanying series of harmonics. These additional and detachable coils were called crooks. By the addition of a suitable crook an alto horn in C (i.e. having C as its fundamental) could be transposed into a horn in F, a fifth lower. Only one series could be played at a time but the composer could indicate which series was the most serviceable and even change in the course of a piece, provided he did not demand the use of an extremely loose lip for low notes and an extremely tight lip for high notes from the same player. He did not however write out the actual notes he wanted, he was content to indicate what crook was to be used—Horn in D, Horn in E flat and so on, and to write in the key of C, as much as to say ' Blow Harmonic No. 5', or whatever it might be. The horn therefore became a transposing instrument and sounds lower than written, the horn in D a seventh, the horn in E flat and E a major and minor sixth respectively, and the horn in F a fifth lower than the notes written for it in the treble clef. A useful dodge for reading a horn in E flat is to treat it as though the part was written in the bass clef with a signature of three flats. Nowadays all horn parts are written in C as though for horns in F. But Brahms always prescribed the precise crooks he needed, although by his time the modern valve horn had come into use. Now that the horn in F is standardized and players play on it parts written for other crooks, transposing them as they go, there is really no reason why the parts should continue to be written in C, and the more rational practice has begun of providing horn parts with a suitably transposed key signature. The valve enabled the hornist to do what the crooks did not, namely change the fundamental length and pitch of his instrument at will. The principle of the valve is the same as that of the crook, namely the insertion of additional lengths of tubing in the main body of the instrument, but instead of these being detachable the extra lengths are built into the instrument and brought into operation by opening valves. Three valves worked by pistons are now to be found on horns, trumpets, cornets and tubas, as well as on the military and brass band instruments, the saxhorns, euphoniums, and their variants. Some conductors specify four-valve horns for use in the orchestra. Sir Thomas Beecham did when he founded the L.P.O. What the valves do is to open in order sufficient lengths of extra tube to depress the pitch by a tone, a half tone and a tone and a half; the fourth valve actually raises the pitch to B flat by cutting out and bypassing some length of pipe, though the fourth valve on the tuba acts in the same direction as the other three and lowers the pitch by two tones and a half. If more than one valve is depressed at a time, the pitch is correspondingly lowered by the sum of their respective intervals, so that if valves 1 and 2 are depressed together the pitch is lowered a tone and a half; but valve No. 3 will also lower the pitch a tone and a half; so that the player has alternative ways of playing the same series of notes, and if he puts all three valves down together he makes available the series three whole tones lower. Three valves thus give the player six extra series of notes—he can now in fact play a chromatic scale in every key.

The horn player has one other resource; by inserting his hand into the bell of his instrument and changing his lip pressure he can raise his notes by a semi-tone and change their tone colour in doing so. These are called stopped notes. Somewhat similarly produced but with greater wind pressure are the brassy (*cuivré*), more blaring notes of the horn. One way and another therefore the horn has broken loose from its natural limitations and can play any notes in its compass in quite a number of different ways. Its artistic status has correspondingly increased, and the improvements in its manufacture now enable a single player to play the whole of the famous solo passage in the Ninth Symphony, which formerly owing to the width of its compass had to be divided between two players, the first and the fourth hornists. The limitations imposed by the player's difficulty in passing from low notes made by a loose lip to high notes made by a tight lip are responsible for the practice of writing for horns in interlocked pairs; Nos. 1 and 3 take the higher notes of the harmony, Nos. 2 and 4 the lower. In spite of the increased flexibility now available this distribution of labour is still observed.

The changes in the instrument have also wrought some change in the character of the music written for it. A good honest arpeggio theme like the opening bars of the Eroica Symphony are typical hand-horn music. In Strauss's *Till Eulenspiegel* Till's motif is an example of what can be done by the addition of chromatic notes, and the tune that opens the slow movement of Tchaikovsky's fifth symphony shows such an extension of its capacity as almost to make it indistinguishable from a viola. It is tempting to draw an analogy from morals. The old-fashioned honest man, blunt in speech and limited in vocabulary, has given way to the clever fellow who can tell any tale; loss of character and gain in intelligence have to be set off against each other. But no one is going to be so reactionary in music, as he is sometimes tempted to be in matters of conduct, as to prefer tiresome if honest stupidity to the quicker wit and greater pliability of smart youth. Blunt speech is even more of a nuisance in music than in daily life.

It is of course true that in art limitations may often prove a source of æsthetic advantage; a sonnet is a sonnet because of the limitations imposed by its metrical scheme, and the exigencies of rhyme may be a potent factor in the creation of poetry, just as the recalcitrance of marble is an element in the greatness of sculpture. One has to be very careful in removing a defect not to remove thereby at the same time the quality which is its obverse. In music the most conspicuous instance of an instrument which is made artistically by its chief defect is the piano. The fundamental characteristic of the piano is the evanescence of its tone; its chief virtue the illusion which it can create of sustained singing. The new electrophonic piano which can not only sustain but even increase the volume of its tone (crescendo on a held chord) is no longer a piano. There is in music (again as in morals) the necessity for overcoming. What one demands of art is not ease but difficulty, and then one can create the illusion of ease—hence all the pleasures of virtuosity.

But we must not allow all this æsthetic purity to blind us to the badness of pre-valve brass instruments. Horns, (more than trumpets), have undergone a change of character since Beethoven's day, and many conductors no longer play the cacophonous introduction to the finale of the Ninth Symphony as the composer wrote it. Weingartner, for instance, used to take the bass soloist at his word when he says " Oh, friends, not thus be our music " and told his brass to double the wood-wind. Such revisions are common practice.

The Trumpet

The trumpet has undergone a somewhat similar change of character for similar reasons. Like the horn it is now a completely chromatic instrument with considerable flexibility of execution. These increased powers have been acquired through the invention of valves, but the modern trumpet differs from the old natural trumpet in other respects, notably length and bore. The trumpet's method of sound production is the same as that of the horn, but it is essentially a soprano instrument with a length of tube half that of the horn, and middle C, the second harmonic, its lowest note. Horns, trumpets and bugles stand to one another as a group of 16-,8-, and 4-foot brass instruments, using organ terminology. The cornet is a connexion of both, for its bore is conical like the horn and bugle but its pitch and crooking is that of the trumpet. Its tone is smoother and less brilliant than the trumpet's, but it is nimbler, speaks more easily and is altogether more melodic— it is the first violin of the brass band. The changes of character that have come over the trumpet have approximated it to the cornet. The cylindrical bore of the trumpet which gives it its brilliance has been modified, so that the modern trumpet, like the cornet, is a better blender than the old natural trumpet which was reserved for the purpose of dominating the score. The change in length has been even more extraordinary. In Bach's time the bore and the mouthpiece (which have a great effect on tone quality and ease of execution) were such that the player could execute the brilliant high trumpet part of the second Brandenburg Concerto, which lies in the fourth octave of its harmonic series. This part is virtually unplayable on the little modern trumpet in B flat or C, and the most far-fetched explanations have been sought for the apparent disappearance of a faculty during a time when instruments have been improved and executive standards have in general been rising. It has however been proved (by Dr. W. G. Whittaker while he was performing Bach's Church Cantatas with the Newcastle Bach Choir) that these high trumpet parts can be played if the player practises a tight lip and abstains from general trumpet playing which involves too much variety of lip tension. The main point however is that old trumpet parts were written to be played in the high register (*i.e.* in the fourth octave of the harmonic series) of a long-tubed instrument, modern trumpet parts to be played in a lower register (corresponding to the third octave of its series) of the shorter, but valvular, chromatic instrument. For the modern trumpet is just half the length of the old, due allowance being made for differences of key.

Up till the middle of the nineteenth century a biggish trumpet in F was built (about six feet long) and it looked as though the trumpet, like the horn, might settle on an F crook as its permanent specification. Players however in their constant search for flexibility were discarding this F trumpet in favour of smaller instruments in A and B flat, and now finally a trumpet in C is becoming the standard instrument in England.

The trumpet is still capable of brilliance, but its chief orchestral purpose now is to form the top part of the brass chorus in symphonic writing. For the performance of works in the polyphonic style in which the trumpeter is a soloist, as in Bach's Brandenburg Concerto, or an obbligatist, as in Handel's bass solo in *The Messiah*, 'The trumpet shall sound', various devices are employed, of which the chief is the adoption of what is misleadingly called a Bach trumpet. This instrument is a product, not of Bach's time, but of the late nineteenth century and was invented by Kosleck of Berlin in 1884 for a literal and unedited performance of Bach's trumpet parts. It is a straight tube like a post-horn fitted with two valves and originally built in A, but later made with three valves in D. This has recently been superseded by an ordinary trumpet built in high D. A specially constructed trumpet in high F was used successfully by Herbert Barr at the Leeds festival of 1922. Thus the short trumpet is now the recognised approach to these difficult parts.

Purists deplore the reduction of parts written for different kinds of trumpets in different keys at different periods to the modern common denominator of a short trumpet in C. It is an example of standardization not elsewhere parallelled in the evolution of the orchestra, and indeed seems to be a move in the opposite direction to the tendency which during the past sixty years or so has sought for ever increasing subtlety and discrimination of tone. The explanation is perhaps to be found in the word 'blend'. The tones of the orchestra have become more various but they must at all costs combine into a homogeneous tutti. The use of the trumpet in jazz bands carries this demilitarization, this robotization of music's most brilliant aggressor, a stage further, and the use of the mute, so fashionable in the fairly recent past, reduces the 'trumpet's loud clangour' to a snigger. Evolution has over-reached itself in the case of that noble savage, the trumpet, and a price has to be paid for the civilising process that has made it a well-behaved co-operator in the orchestral team-spirit.

THE CORNET

The cornet has always been despised as plebeian for just these accommodating qualities. It has however found favour in

French scores ever since the time when it was invented about 1830. In England its chief use has been in theatre orchestras and brass bands. It ought not to be regarded as a substitute for the trumpet, for its tone lacks the ring of heroism which even now the trumpet retains. If there is rarely a distinctive niche for it in the symphony orchestra, its flexibility, blendability and moderate brassiness make it an extremely useful member of a theatre band, not so much as a substitute for the trumpet as a partner for the clarinet.

THE TROMBONE

The trombones are natural counterparts of lower pitch of the trumpet and the name itself is Italian for big trumpet. The German is *Posaune* and in old English the instrument is known as the sackbut. Sackbut itself is derived from the Spanish for a draw-pipe (or pump) and is descriptive of the characteristic feature of the trombone, which is the moveable slide. By means of the slide the length of the tube is changed at will and the pitch correspondingly varied, so that all the mechanism of crooks and valves is rendered unnecessary *ab initio*. Nothing in fact could be simpler nor musically more efficient, for a complete harmonic series is given from any position of the slide and the player makes his own notes at the guidance of his ear, as a violinist does. There are seven recognized ' positions ', each extension giving a fundamental note a semi-tone lower than the next shorter position. The now obsolete alto trombone had as its lowest note (the second harmonic) in the closed position E flat on the bass stave, the tenor trombone has the B flat below, and the bass trombone the G on the bottom line. The seven semi-tone extensions give a further diminished fifth below in each case. An incidental advantage of these positions is that they afford the player alternative ways of producing the same note, either as a high harmonic of a low fundamental, or as not so high a harmonic of a not so low fundamental. Good trombone playing consists in not working the pump-handle too hard, but in finding short cuts between consecutive notes of the music by varying the lip tension.

The tone is rich in quiet playing, brilliant in loud and overwhelmingly powerful in a fortissimo. Three is the normal number employed, two tenors and a bass, and they are used as a chorus. Sometimes the bass trombone may be used without its fellows for reinforcement of the main bass lines, but solos are rarely satisfactory, as may be ascertained in any performance of Mozart's *Requiem*, where a tenor trombone obbligato in the " Tuba Mirum " sounds like a bad cornet player outside a public house round the corner.   The instrument came into the symphony orchestra from the opera, where it was used for effects of special solemnity by both Gluck and Mozart, and by Beethoven, who was responsible for introducing a trio of them into symphonic music for the more generalized purpose of adding weight and power to the total ensemble.

An interesting case of its dramatic use outside opera and symphony is in Mendelssohn's oratorio, *Elijah*, where the Lord only answers the Prophet's prayers when they are reinforced (at the third time of supplication) with trombones.   Incidentally *Elijah* begins with a characteristic chord for trombones heralding Elijah's proclamation of the three-year's drought.   Another example of characterization apart from the stage is the bold phrase for trombones in unison depicting the oriental despot in Rimsky-Korsakov's suite *Scheherezade*.   This decisive tone-quality the trombone owes to its combination of a cylindrical with a conical bore (and, as always in brass instruments, a suitably corresponding mouthpiece).   It is cylindrical like a trumpet for most of its length but where the bell-joint turns the last corner the tube flares conically to the bell.   The fundamentals of the first three positions on the trombones can just be produced with a loose embouchure and are known as pedal notes.   Berlioz describes them as " enormous and magnificent on the tenor trombone, of indifferent sonorousness on the alto trombone, and terrible on the bass trombone when they can be got out ".   The tenor trombone is the most generally useful member of the family and has found a new sphere of operations in jazz bands.   Jazz which vulgarizes (in both senses) everything it touches, makes great play with the trombone's power of glissando, for it is one of the ironies of its nature that it cannot play a true legato but can portamento for almost any distance at any rate of slither.

THE TUBA

The general function of the tuba is to act as the contra-bass of the heavy brass group, to underline the bass trombone often at an octave below.   Its tone however does not really blend with trombones and trumpets—they are sharp and it is blunt. It owes its present place in the orchestra more to its general utility in this contra-bass role, in place of the unsatisfactory serpents and ophicleides and other monsters, than to any natural congruity with orchestral sound. Its superior utility it owes to the fact that it can play its open (fundamental) note and with the aid of its four valves every chromatic semi-tone between it and its octave—it has in fact a complete bottom octave— unlike the trombones whose pedal notes leave a gap of half an octave unfilled. This command of the open note it owes to a wider bore than the horns and trumpets have. In military circles there are three instruments of this design—the euphonium a tenor, a bombardon or bass tuba in E flat, which if built in circular form to be crossed over the shoulder for ease of carriage on the march is called a helicon, and a contra-bass bombardon in B flat below. The concert orchestra has borrowed the second of these and rebuilt it in F. The tenor instrument is found however in orchestral scores. Strauss uses a tenor tuba (*i.e.* a euphonium) to portray the loutish character of Sancho Panza and Holst, who also has exceptional feeling for brass instruments, sometimes uses it, notably at the beginning of *The Planets* to portray the grim brutality of Mars. The special Wagner tubas, so called, are a family of five extra brass instruments which Wagner specified for *The Ring*, just as he did an extra bass trumpet. His designs however had to be modified in practice, and opera houses vary in the methods they employ to carry out his intentions. What he wanted was a tone colour between the horns and the tubas and he prescribed a conical bore intermediate between the two. Four of his special tubas were really therefore modified horns, and Hermann Scherchen in his book on conducting recommends that the regular horn players should keep their hands (and lips) in practice on them instead of fetching in military players from outside for them. In this country we more often get trombonists to play the specially made instruments, which are modified saxhorns. The fifth contra-bass tuba was a true tuba and offers no special difficulty.

The bombardon is now the recognised contra-bass of the military band (*i.e.* reed and brass), of the brass band, (an all-brass combination which enjoys great popularity in this country among industrial workers), and, in the form of the tuba in F, of the symphony orchestra. This alignment came about gradually during the last century, but there is still a great variety of pattern among all these brass instruments and great confusion of nomenclature. The inventions of Adolphe Sax were a powerful stimulus to the brass-band movement in this country, and that in turn has maintained an interest in the possibilities and improvement of all these brass instruments which depend for their tone production upon the harmonic series of an open reedless pipe. As far as the orchestra is concerned however none but the bass tuba has acquired a permanent footing in it, though occasional visitors are invited by composers for special purposes.

III. PERCUSSION

This brings us to the end of the brass group and leads to a consideration of the percussion department. Two main classes of instruments are employed; those that give out notes of a definite pitch—timpani, glockenspiel, xylophone, tubular bells, celesta, and those of a purely rhythmic nature—drum, bass-drum, tambourine, cymbals, gong (tam-tam), triangle and castanets. The jazz band has added a few more to this battery —the Chinese block, slapstick, the wire brush as a striker. Composers sometimes call for special contrivances, like the wind machine, the anvil, and the rattle, for special effects.

THE TIMPANI

Of this motley company the only instrument of serious and permanent musical value, an integral part of the texture and not a mere decoration upon it, is the set of kettle-drums with their notes of definite pitch and their capacity for fine nuances of tone and expression. Drums are found in orchestral scores as early as Purcell but not in Monteverde. A pair of them sufficed until Beethoven's day; thereafter three became common form (though Brahms, an economical scorer, was content with two), while spendthrifts like Berlioz, Wagner and Mahler sometimes demanded six, *i.e.* two complete parts with a player for each. Their function is not only rhythmic but harmonic, and in classical scores up to the time of Beethoven they are generally though not invariably tuned to the tonic and dominant of the key of the piece, with the dominant assigned to the larger drum a fourth below the tonic. More varied tunings were introduced by Beethoven, and with three drums regularly available considerable freedom in the use of unessential notes became available to the composer, but the nature of the instrument is against its use across the harmony; its function is to clarify by a stroke of emphasis not to create confusion by an assertion of irrelevance. The invention of mechanically tuned drums was a temptation to write parts including many chromatic or unessential notes but perhaps because they thus go against the natural genius of the instrument they have not succeeded in driving out the hand-tuned drums.

The name of the orchestral drums in English is kettle-drums, in Italian timpani. By a common mistake side-drums are often ignorantly called kettle-drums. Perhaps the word kettle suggests by false onomatopœa the rattle of the snares of a side-drum. The kettle in question is a cauldron, the three-legged variety commonly used by witches, or what housewives who do their washing at home would call a copper. Timpani, the books say, should be spelt so, and not with a Y, because there is no letter Y in the Italian alphabet, but any one with even a smattering of the classics will find it difficult not to write tympani, since the word is pure Greek and is transliterated into Latin with a Y, but it must be conceded that for consistency of derivation it should make a plural *tympana* instead of *tympani*. The German is *Pauken* and the French *timbales*.

There is a hole in the bottom of the kettle to let out the excess of vibration; the top is covered by a skin called a head and generally made of calf; round the circumference is a row of taps which are the tuning keys regulating the tension of the head and consequently the pitch of the note. One of these keys is detachable so as to allow the drummer unimpeded access to the surface of his drum at the best point of impact, which is not in the middle of the skin but about a handsbreadth in from the circumference. It is important to get the drum tuned evenly all over, otherwise the tone suffers. The sticks are of cane covered with felt. English drummers are not nearly careful enough to have sticks with heads of different hardness. There is available an extreme range of dry crackle from the wooden end of the drumstick to soft rumble from a sponge-headed stick and at all degrees of loudness. The famous passage in the thirteenth 'Enigma' Variation, where Mendelssohn's *Prosperous Voyage* is quoted by the clarinet, is accompanied by a pianissimo roll executed with the wrong end of the drumstick, and it is possible to produce quite a loud and voluminous sound from a soft-headed stick. Most English drummers are content with a single pair or at most two pairs of sticks but the Berlin Philharmonic drummer brings a whole case-full on to the platform. The Bournemouth drummer of the last twenty years shows more appreciation of the subleties of drumming than any other English drummer whom I have observed. Conductors do not pay enough attention to the matter and often permit fortissimo passages to swamp the rest of the orchestra. Without any abatement of tone this need not happen if the drums were to be put on the floor among the other instruments, instead of being elevated above and behind their fellows on raised tiers, from which their sound comes straight out over the strings and wood-wind without blending with them. Theatre arrangements are much better in this respect and the notes of the drum, however loud, pick up the harmonic bass and vibrate sympathetically with the orchestral tutti. In the concert hall too often even a tutti is extinguished in a drum solo.

When there were only two drums they divided the octave F to F between them. With the addition of a third intermediate drum they are now expected to reach a tone further in either direction. Thus Elgar in the 'Troyte' Variation writes a brilliant solo for three drums on G C G, and low E is not uncommonly written for the largest drum. Beethoven had originally made use of an octave tuning in the Eight and Ninth Symphonies. Other conspicuous drum parts in Beethoven are the reiterated crotchets at the beginning of the Violin Concerto and the solo passage which is only the culmination of an extremely important drum part in the lyrical slow movement of the Fourth Symphony. A chord of the fifth played on two drums simultaneously sounds well. Berlioz writes a chord of four notes and a sustained double roll in his Requiem. In the slow movement of the Fantastic Symphony he prescribes four drums and a player for each, since a four-part chord has to be rolled. Stravinsky in *Le Sacre du Printemps* puts an elaborate ostinato on two sets of timpani. But in general the kettledrums serve two main purposes ; to strike single notes for rhythmic and harmonic emphasis and to roll either loud or soft for the opposite purpose of blurring the outlines of the music with a soft quilt of sound.

DRUMS

The bass drum has an even bigger surface (as a rule) than the big kettle-drum and is struck with a heavier stick with a larger padded head. Its note has no definite pitch but being vaguely low appears to have, in such a context as the baritone solo, " Mors stupebit ", in Verdi's Requiem. It acts as a deep bass by sympathetic vibration in such a movement as Sibelius's *En Saga*, where it combines with bass strings more sonorously than would the timpani, which are deliberately excluded from the score. Rolls can be played on it for mysterious effect by a pair of timpani sticks. Crude effects of battle have been employed by composers as respectable as Beethoven in his *Battle of Vittoria* and Tchaikovsky in his *1812 Overture*, and simple military march rhythm is an obviously legitimate use of the big drum. But sparing use and gentle handling have an artistic effect in inverse ratio to direct onslaught. The first appearance of big drum, cymbals, and triangle as a consort of percussion in symphonic music is in two movements of Haydn's ' Military ' symphony in which they are decorously used. An allegretto movement in march rhythm takes the place of a slow movement and in the presto finale in $\frac{6}{8}$ time the extra instruments lend a touch of frank gaiety.

The side-drum, which is the mainstay of Church Lads' Brigade and other drum and fife bands, finds a more restricted use in the orchestra, except for its proud heraldic purpose in announcing ' The King '. Its characteristic rattle is produced by the snares which double the dry beat of the two wooden sticks. These snares are strings of gut (varying in number according to the drummers' fancy) stretched diagonally across the under surface of this drum, which has two parchment membranes to vibrate. The impact on the top head sends a wave of air through the the cylindrical body of the drum and pushes the lower head outward to strike against the snares. The player holds his sticks in such a way as to get two blows from each stroke—stroke and its rebound from each hand alternately. One double stroke from each hand thus gives a continuous crackle of eight sharp sounds. By this generous multiplication a quick-firing rattle is produced, though the technique of an even and well controlled roll is not easy to acquire. I remember being confronted at a competition festival in an ' own choice ' instrumental class with a quartet of drums from a Boys' Brigade

(two of them side-drums, one tenor drum and one bass drum)
who pitted themselves against a string quartet and a pianoforte
trio. They were easily the best performers but I did not feel
quite justified in placing them above the other competitors,
who although inferior executants were more tuneful in total
musical effect. ' Paradiddle ', ' flam ' and ' ruff ' are technical
names of certain ways of beating rhythmic groups.

The tenor drum is a large two-headed side drum without
snares.

Indian drums played by the fingers are too delicate for use
in Western orchestras, but may be seen and heard in various
gourd-like shapes and sizes in the orchestra of Indian instruments with which Mr. Uday Shankar accompanies his
dances.

The tabor, which is a small drum traditionally played with a
pipe by a single player, has been revived along with folk-dancing,
to which it is a traditional accompaniment. The one-man band
holds a three-hole pipe in the left hand from which the tabor
dangles and holds a drum stick in the right. This sort of tabor
may be no more than a small tambourine without jingles, or it
may be a small double-headed side-drum with a single mild
snare. Bizet has prescribed a tabor in *L'Arlésienne*.

The tambourine (tambour Basque) is a single-headed drum
fitted with tiny pairs of cymbals let into its rim. It can be
struck, shaken or rubbed with the thumb. Its effect is immediately to suggest peasant dancing from sunny climes—Arab,
Italian, Spanish and gypsy. But it appears in so grand and
dignified a score as Elgar's second symphony. It is an easy
instrument to start up but less easy to silence promptly.

THE BATTERY

The triangle, cymbals and gong emit euphonious sounds,
but so rich in harmonics that they have no definite pitch and
will go with, while refusing to combine with, anything. Their
purpose is rhythmic and colouristic. The triangle is a bent
steel rod struck with a straight rod of the same material. It can
be trilled if the beater is shaken across one of the angles, and
can thus be used to put fire into a climax. But an even more
striking effect of climax is secured by Wagner's first single stroke
in the *Meistersinger* Overture. Brahms the reticent uses it
quite extensively in the Scherzo of his fourth symphony and

Liszt raises it to the eminence of a solo in his E flat piano concerto (the " Infernal Triangle " concerto). Haydn, of course, has a part for it in his Toy Symphony and also a more substantial and serious one in the ' Military' symphony which he wrote for the Salomon Concerts in London.

The cymbals ought not to be attached to the big drum—it spoils their tone. What is good enough for a circus is not good enough for the orchestra. Besides, there are other uses for them than merely clashing them together. They can be touched off quietly against each other ; they can be played with a kettledrum stick ; they can be rolled edgewise against each other with a tinkling cymbal effect. Military bands and orchestras use large cymbals, but dancers have recently revived more delicate kinds, and Stravinsky in *Le Sacre du Printemps* and Debussy in *L'Après-midi d'un Faune* follow Berlioz (in the " Queen Mab " scherzo of his " Romeo " symphony and in *Les Troyens*) in employing more refined Oriental cymbals of this kind. Drum and cymbal effects, when introduced into the orchestra by Mozart in *Seraglio*, were also intended to create an oriental atmosphere—Turkish music in fact to suit the drama. Beethoven, however, when he followed suit in the finale of the Ninth Symphony seems to have been aiming at a touch of the grotesque, on the gargoyle principle, in order to realize the sublime. A crash on the cymbal solo marks the opening of Till Eulenspiegel's ride through the market place and the discomfiture of the traders in Strauss's symphonic poem.

The gong (tam-tam) is used rather as a super-triangle for one-note effects. The player may be observed girding himself to deliver his one master-stroke at the climax. There is an instance of an electrifying note from the gong in *The Dream of Gerontius* at the moment when the Demons first appear upon the scene. It contributes persistent rolls to the noise of war in Holst's " Mars ". Less restrained use for the sake of local colour is to be found in *Madame Butterfly*.

Glockenspiel, celesta, xylophone and tubular bells form a group of instruments, struck with hammers, that are capable of melody. All are brightly toned and are therefore effective in inverse ratio to the frequency and duration of their employment.

The present form of glockenspiel and xylophone are similarly constructed instruments standardized to twenty-seven chromatic notes, the one made of steel plates, the other of wooden blocks, both mounted on resonators and struck with two wooden hammers. The glockenspiel is a tiny carillon sounding at a dizzy height. Wagner uses it both in the *Ring* and in *Meistersinger* to fringe with an outline of intense brightness an already high snatch of tune on wood-wind. There is an enchanting movement for carillon in Handel's *Saul*, and Papageno carries and plays his own small glockenspiel in the *Magic Flute*, the counterpart of Tamino's flute given him by the three Ladies. In Holst's " Mercury " glockenspiel and celesta play together, the one picking out a diamond-like rhythm and the other interjecting soft chords among it.

The xylophone has a more barbaric flavour and a more specialised application. Examples of its use are in Saint-Saens's *Danse Macabre* and in Lambert's *Rio Grande*, where it accompanies the words " Loud is the Marimba's note ". It is also used as part of the general battery in Holst's " Uranus ".

The celesta is a keyboard instrument the size of a harmonium but employing hammers like a piano's to strike steel plates whose tone is enhanced by wooden resonators. It is a modern invention, contrived by Mustel of Paris in 1886, but has attained a wide use in modern scores. It has a compass of four octaves and sounds an octave higher than written. Its purity of tone enables it to pick out a melody like a more delicate glockenspiel, or to play little solos and decorative passages. It will play fairy-like arpeggios and even harmony by the handful does not come amiss to it, as appears in Tchaikovsky's *Casse-Noisette Suite* where it accompanies a solo from the bass clarinet. Rachmaninov uses it extensively and in varied ways in *The Bells*, and Strauss in *Der Rosenkavalier* assigns to it the theme of the presentation of the rose.

Castanets, like the xylophone, are made of resonant wood but they are purely rhythmic in function. These clicking pieces of wood held in the palms of the hands are mostly used to give Spanish local colour and can hardly be said to be permanently acclimatized to the orchestra. They are of oriental origin, brought into Spain by the Moors, and now suggest by infallible association Spanish dance rhythms. Naturally they turn up in Ravel's *Bolero* and in Bizet's *Carmen*. French composers, it should be noticed, are fond of writing Spanish music.

Speaking generally all percussion instruments are capable of more discriminating playing than they normally get in English symphony orchestras. Since their function is mainly decorative there is no reason why they should not invariably perform it with exquisite elegance. Constant Lambert gives a lead towards greater discrimination and care in his specification of percussion and the instruction therewith in his *Rio Grande*. He prescribes five players for the following instruments : xylophone, jeu de timbre, (=keyed glockenspiel), triangle, castanets, small cowbell (without clapper), tambourine, side-drum, tenor drum, Chinese tomtom, Chinese block, cymbals, Turkish crash (one large suspended cymbal), bass drum, tam-tam, three timpani. He adds a note to the effect that the side-drum player should be provided with a wire brush as used in jazz bands, and in the score he indicates further refinements of execution which, he is emphatic, must be carried out meticulously —such as rolling timpani with the finger nails, with sponge-headed-sticks, with wooden-headed sticks ; he marks some cymbal notes *laissez vibrer* and others *étouffez*, and he advocates a separate rehearsal for the percussion department in the cadenza which it shares with the solo pianist.

The old attitude was to lump all these percussion instruments together and call them, by a confused derivation from the French, " kitchen furniture " or in abbreviation simply " kitchen ". They are now called to higher responsibilities and it is more respectful to call them collectively " the battery ". In this department an example of greater refinement has been provided by jazz players. One may not expect refinement from jazz, but its treatment of percussion has been more subtle than anything to be found in ' straight ' orchestral music.

IV. STRINGS

THE HARP

The harp part stands between the percussion and the violins in an orchestral score, a position which corresponds precisely to its intermediate character, for the harp is a stringed instrument percussively operated. That plucking is a form of striking may be seen in the harpsichord where the keys of a keyboard move a lever on which is mounted a quill. When the key is depressed the lever jumps up and thrusts the quill against and past the string from underneath ; and the impact of the quill on the wire and its release are characteristic of the attack of the harpsichord. The harp, however, has less bite than the harpsichord, because instead of a sharp quill on a wooden lever the string is set into vibration by the soft pad of the player's fingers. In fact the harp is an instrument for the production of an extended and amplified string pizzicato, and its tone quality is definitely stringy, for its forty-seven strings like those of the violins and violoncellos, are of gut, the lower ones 'covered' or 'wound' with wire like the lower strings of the violin family. But its percussive character and its harmonic limitations, which are due to its construction, keep it outside the string family and it maintains a certain isolation on the border where those other hybrids, the piano and the organ, pitch their tents when they enter the orchestral domain. The position of the harp is ambiguous also from another point of view—that of history. It is one of the oldest of instruments and it is one of the newcomers (just preceding the saxophone) to the orchestra. In essentials the harp and its music are unchanged from the most ancient times, but the mechanism which made possible its entry into the modern orchestra, with its requirements of chromatic harmony and wide modulation, is the work of Sebastian Erard who produced his double-action harp in 1810.

The double action consists of a set of seven pedals, one for each note of the diatonic scale, which can be depressed either one or two notches. The first notch raises all the strings of its denomination one semi-tone; double action, or depression into the second notch, raises them a further semi-tone. The harp is built in C flat. When the C pedal is depressed all the C flats on the instrument become C naturals; depression into the second notch converts C naturals into C sharps by shortening the strings still further. Similarly for D, E, F, G, A and B. This mechanism enables the player by a suitable combination of pedal actions to produce the same note from two consecutive strings, and the playing of repeated notes is one legitimate and characteristic feature of the harp's technique. Chords, like dominant and diminished sevenths, can also be 'set' by manipulation of the pedal, and the harp's most spectacular performance is the dashing execution of such chords *glissando* by sweeping the arms through some six octaves. It can also perform isolated notes as octave harmonics by stopping the string in the right place with the base of the thumb. Normally it plays chords in close position or in arpeggio form.

The harp in its simpler manifestations has appeared inter-mittently all through modern music (*i.e.* from the end of the sixteenth century onwards). It is found in Monteverde's orchestra where a double (not double-action) harp is specified. It is found in the score of Handel's *Giulio Cesare* and its use was invoked for special effects in the theatre. Mozart wrote for it a concerto with flute, and Beethoven specified a harp for his *Prometheus* music. But the modern full-size harp was given orchestral status by Wagner and Berlioz. The latter discusses it quite coldly in his *Modern Instrumentation* but uses it to some purpose in *La Damnation de Faust*. The advent of the sym-phonic poem established it in the symphony orchestra, where two harps are now a recognised part of the establishment.

THE VIOLIN FAMILY

The violins, violas, violoncellos and contrabasses that make up the great family of strings which is the backbone, mainstay and chief executive of the orchestra, may be generically des-cribed before their characters are severally analysed. They reached perfection in one stride, after a long evolution in pri-mitive form through the Middle Ages, in the Italian workshops at Cremona in the mid-sixteenth century. Viols and violins were made concurrently but the only influence left on the modern orchestra by the old viols was the three-stringed bass which was really a violone. Common to them all is the excitation of their strings by a horse-hair bow. This bow took longer to reach its present form, in which the stick is slightly arched inwards towards the hair and not convexly as in an archer's bow, than the violin did to find its true shape. But the bowing technique with its many refinements and devices is responsible for the distinctive character of string playing—its sustained, singing tone, its extreme sensitiveness to the pressure of the wrist and consequent dynamic range, its swishing impetus when many violins execute a lively passage with identical bowing, its mer-curial response to the slightest nuance of expression, its rhyth-mic energy derived from the to-and-fro motion of the bow across the strings. Up bows and down bows differ in attack ; the tremolo produces quick reiteration of the same note or notes in an excited manner by means of rapid oscillation of the bow ; phrasing is shaped by grouping notes together in one pull of the bow or by detaching a single note and giving it a stroke to itself; the bow may hammer the strings *martellato*, or it may jump lightly on it *saltato*, or it may turn itself over and play *col legno* (*i.e.* with the wood). This little catalogue does not exhaust the resources of this curiously simple yet by no means obvious piece of mechanism for exciting sound waves from strings, resources which are astonishingly large and varied and of extreme subtlety.

The method of sound production common to the whole violin family was discovered at least as long ago as the time of Pythagoras, who carried out his acoustic experiments and calculations on a monochord consisting of a string stretched on a bridge over a resonating soundboard. The tension of the string may be varied to produce notes of different pitch, and violinists tune their fiddles by screwing the strings up and down on pegs that vary their tension though not their vibrating length; but what Pythagoras discovered was that pitch varied with the length of string. Length and tension are the interlocking-factors governing pitch. The actual production of tone is to be explained as follows—a string is pulled out of the straight by a finger or plectrum, the natural elasticity of the gut (or metal) causes it to spring back beyond the straight and then to oscillate to and fro until it comes to a standstill. The whole of the string therefore describes an ellipse and causes an equivalent disturbance in the air by pushing the air particles in and out. These air vibrations are regular and periodic—the period depending on the length of the string, the air surrounding the string being alternately compressed and rarified.

If the string is plucked there is only the one initial impulse imparted to the string, and as the vibrations decrease in amplitude (though not in frequency) the sound dies away. But if the bow is applied to the string the pushing and pulling action is continuous and not transitory. The rosin on the bow sticks to the strings and pulls it to one side until the tension of the string overcomes the friction of the bow and the string slips. It will rebound just as it did when plucked, but on its return journey as the tension of the string wanes and the friction of the bow once more accumulates, the bow will again pull at the string and cause the vibrations to continue with undiminished vigour. The amplitude of the vibrations is maintained and with them the volume of tone. The tone quality depends not on the amplitude, which accounts for the power, nor on the frequency, which accounts for the pitch, but on the shape of the sound waves. The curve of the violin waves as traced by a phonodeik is very regular and has an affinity with that of the human voice. The intimacy of control exercised by the bow is more immediate than in any other instrument. These two bonds between the instrument and its player give to the violin a specially human appeal. The combination of many violins playing together makes a partnership of a specially close communion. When the violas, violoncellos and basses join the group in appropriate numerical proportions and so make a complete harmony and a homogeneous texture, there is developed a corporate personality which is the nucleus for uniting in one grand corporation all the players of other instruments who are less continuously in action. But there is a curious distinction, both of tone and of ethos, between a solo violin and a number of violins playing in unison. A solo violin will stand out quite clearly from an accompaniment of several violins. A mere doubling of the four string parts is not enough to turn a quartet into a string band, but double them again and you have something like the characteristic sound of strings in consort. The explanation generally offered for this difference in tone colour, in so far as it is not a case of the familiar difference between the individual in his individuality and the individual acting in a team, is that minute differences of intonation, which the ear readily fuses, give a more massive, a less pure, a richer sound than the individual violin in isolation.

It is convenient to remember the lowest notes of each of the string instruments as a guide to its compass and tuning. The lowest open string of the violin sounds tenor G below middle C, the viola's bottom string is one fifth lower *i.e.* baritone C, and the violoncello's lowest note is the C an octave below that. All three instruments tune their strings in fifths. The double bass differs from the rest of the family in tuning its strings in fourths. It also sometimes indulges in the luxury of a fifth string which takes its compass down to the C an octave below that of the violoncello, whereby it is able to play the violoncello parts of classical symphonies in which the two instruments run together, playing the same part at an octave's distance. Thus in playing Beethoven's symphonies on an ordinary bass it is sometimes necessary to break back into a higher octave when the part runs below E, which is the bottom note of the four-stringed bass. Modern music from *Parsifal* onwards sometimes demands this extension of the compass but the use of five-stringed basses is by no means general.

Ordinary orchestral practice is to divide the body of the violins into two sections playing separate parts corresponding to the soprano and alto voices. The first violins bear the responsibility for the main melodic line of the music. The violinist at the first desk immediately to the left of the conductor's stand is the leader not only of his own department but of the whole orchestra. His special functions are to act as liaison between conductor and players, to play all violin solos, to give a ruling at the conductor's invitation on matters of string technique such as bowing and phrasing, and to be generally responsible for the observance of good manners, professional etiquette and general discipline both at rehearsal and on the platform. These duties he inherits from the days when he was even more important than he is now. Before the nineteenth century he *was* the conductor (except in the theatre or in church), and he is still called *Konzertmeister* in German. He gave the signs to start and stop, and he controlled the tempo, the rhythm and the dynamics. His position was in fact rather like that of the stroke of an eight-oared racing crew. In an opera or oratorio the general superintendence of the performance was, however, not with him but with the player of the harpsichord or piano, who controlled the singers, and the leader's task, then as now, was to keep the players in line with them. When conducting with a baton became the regular practice—Spohr made the innovation in England in 1820—the leader found a subtler task awaiting him. He developed almost telepathic powers of communication with those behind and around him. A good orchestral leader thus makes it easy for a conductor to realize his intentions, and many an inexperienced or incompetent conductor has been saved from overt disaster by an experienced and skilful leader.

Some modern anti-romantic composers like Stravinsky, finding the violin altogether too passionate an instrument, have excluded it from their scores, and it is noteworthy that the hard-boiled jazz band does not base its internal economy on a quartet of strings and only retains a solo violin on sufferance occasionally. Violins have been excluded before now for quite other reasons—Bach for instance in the sixth Brandenburg Concerto gives his two top lines to violas—since the elimination of violins changes the colour as well as the texture of a work.

The violas have come up in the world.   Till the latter part of the eighteenth century they were treated as hacks to fill in the harmony with parts simple enough for incompetent violinists to undertake.   They are now required to be as agile as the violins and there are a certain number of outstanding parts for them ; in Berlioz's *Harold in Italy* the solo viola is of concerto rank and in Strauss's *Don Quixote* the viola must be equal to impersonating Sancho Panza.

The violoncellos normally carry the main bass harmony, but their striking quality as singers of melody may obtain for them the enunciation of a second subject tune, as in Brahms's second symphony (first movement), and (with the horns) in the first movement of the same composer's fourth symphony.   Verdi had a feeling for the darker hues of the violoncello and pictures some of the melodramatic villainy of *Rigoletto* by subdividing the cellos and writing for them in four-part harmony.[1]

The double-bass rarely steps out of the chorus, as violins, violas and violoncellos are constantly doing in many more ways than I have just instanced.   Two such places may be mentioned from opera : in Strauss's *Salome* the head of John the Baptist is severed with a sickening stroke of the bass in a high position, and in Puccini's *Gianni Schicchi* it participates in the shedding of crocodile tears.[1]

The string consort (generally in five parts) on its own account is finding increasing favour to-day.   Mr. Boyd Neel led the way in compiling a repertory consisting of things from the eighteenth century, of which Mozart's *Eine kleine Nachtmusik* is typical, out-of-the-way and mostly short pieces from every period, of which some of Purcell's many Chaconnes are representative, and modern works by the younger generation of composers, of which Benjamin Britten's Simple Symphony may be taken as representative but not typical.   The medium in spite of its superficial resemblance to the string quartet is most happily employed in music of shorter span than three and four movements.   Some big works of spacious design have however been written for an enlargement of the string band into six, eight or more parts.   Such are Elgar's splendid Introduction and Allegro for string quartet and string orchestra (see Concerto Grosso) and Bliss's Music for Strings.

[1] *See Appendix II.*

CHAPTER V

SYMPHONIC FORM

AN orchestra performs three public functions, two of them in association with voices, the other independently in pursuit of its own ends. From the beginning of time instruments have been assembled to adorn and solemnify religious observance ; almost equally ancient is their association with the theatre. The adjectives 'religious' and ' dramatic' may be used in the broadest possible sense to cover every kind of ceremonial and festive occasion when instruments are played in association with voices. In church it may be only a few strings with clarinet and serpent (or bassoon) to support rural hymn-singing, as described by Thomas Hardy and as once practised in many an English village church, but it is an orchestral accompaniment just as surely as the solo violin and flutes in the *Benedictus* of Beethoven's *Mass in D* are an orchestral adjunct to an episcopal ceremony. Actually Beethoven's Mass missed the occasion of its composition, which was an Archbishop's installation in 1820. It was too late and it grew too big, and so it passed into the category of concert oratorios which generically belong to 'religious' music. Nor need the orchestra's ' religious' usages be specifically Christian ; Mozart's Freemasonry Cantatas and Delius's defiantly pagan *Mass of Life* equally call for the highest services the orchestra can render. In short, secular cantatas, biblical oratorios, Catholic masses, church cantatas, humble carols and itinerant waits equally represent one great class of service which the orchestra renders to the community.

Dramatically music ranges from incidental fanfares, marches and dances in a stage-play to a complete cycle of music dramas by Richard Wagner, from the entr'acte which lubricates the passage of the audience from its stalls to the bar to the continuous background of a film. In opera itself the orchestra may do little more than thrum the ' big guitar' of some Italian opera or it may be used with the utmost subtlety to touch in a psychological situation. Many, perhaps most, of the increases in the expressive powers of the orchestra have been acquired in the theatre. Opera is essentially a vocal art, and, in despite of Wagner, the main interest must lie on the stage and in the voice part ; the orchestra is subservient, but the importance of its contribution to the total effect must not be overlooked.

But in a book on the orchestra the main emphasis must be on what it does in its own right, on its own achievements, on its own unaided satisfactions. Symphony, even more than oratorio and opera, is the glory of the orchestra. The symphony evolved during the same period as the orchestra which was to play it, and on parallel lines. The parallel lines, however, with mathematical impropriety converged during the eighteenth century and met in Haydn. The ground-plan of the symphony is that of sonata form, which was evolved principally by experiments in writing for the key-board ; the same principles which enabled longer flights of unaccompanied instrumental music to be made on the harpsichord were applied to concerted music of the home (*i.e.* chamber music with strings) and to the concerted public music of the orchestra. The problem of instrumental music is that of the swimmer and the aviator—how to keep itself up over any considerable distance. Simple tunes such as a piper plays for dancing are constantly coming to cadences, and cadences mean falling places. Early instrumental music is a series of short hops and forced landings. Even in the vocal music of Palestrina and his contemporaries, where the words relieve the composer of his structural problems, the phrases are constantly coming to earth at cadences which are nicely contrived to give varying degrees of finality or of fresh starting. As music developed, more particularly as a sense of key was established in people's minds, the cadences were felt less as terminal points and more as breathing places. In fact, like punctuation points which break up the flow of language, cadences enabled longer sentences to be uttered. And it is length—and, to borrow a ghostly word, levitation—which an instrumental composer desires to achieve. The symphony of Haydn represents the successful issue of a long series of attempts to say something in music without words, of substantial length with just enough repetition of the material (more crudely, the tunes) to give the pleasure of recognition and familiarity and not too much to cause satiety and weariness. It was accomplished by means of melodic pattern, cadence, key and structure. These are all technical terms (of which by far the most important is key) and they form the subject-matter of the countless books on Musical Appreciation which have been written since the lay public began to take an intelligent interest in instrumental music over and above its æsthetic and somewhat passive enjoyment of it. It is the inescapable duty of an author who is commending, and even explaining, orchestral music to ensure that his readers know what a symphony is, and it is inevitable that in tracing the evolution of the symphony technical terms will be used—the only alternative to blunt technical terms is unwieldy circumlocutions. Sonata form has been described in a thousand text-books, but it is essential that not only its formulae but its æsthetic principles should be grasped if any true appreciation of symphony and concerto is to be won. I have already let slip a sketch of what happened in the process of transforming a short and simple dance tune into a long and complicated symphony (Chapter II p. 13). With this apology for a pedagogic manner in what aimed at being a companionable book I will elaborate my sketch and, like Darwin, describe the origin of a species.

The musical equivalent of gravitation in the physical world is tonality, or the propensity of the ear (which is the musician's name for that part of his mind which deals with his aural experience) to relate all the sounds that strike upon it to a centre. This tonal centre is called the tonic. I believe this to be a basic psychological fact and I believe therefore that the attempts of the atonal school of composers to emancipate their music from a tonal centre of gravity and to maintain a strict equality of interest between all twelve notes of the chromatic scale are doomed to failure. Tones will not form themselves into a significant pattern without reference to a tonic; they remain detached sounds and refuse to coalesce into an intelligible pattern. The tonic itself however is not given in nature; it can be any tone you choose; A is not a better tonic than C, nor do 522 vibrations a second give a better centre than 225. In other words there is no absolute tonic; you make your own, but having chosen it you stick to it as your norm, your point of reference, your home port, which has moreover a dynamic pull drawing you constantly to it.

Actually you do not choose a tonic except in so far as you pitch your voice to a definite note before you begin to sing a tune. But any tune you sing will have a tonal centre. It will also show other signs of organization. Organization is the essence of musical form; music is in fact organized sound and, since in its essential nature it is as fleeting as time itself, the mind must find some system of organizing the evanescent experience as it flows past the ear. How can one organize a long piece of string, all length and no thickness? Only by measuring pieces off, and our first measure is memory. Hence repetition or recapitulation is a basic constructive principle of music; recognition of and taking pleasure in the same tune endlessly repeated is characteristic of most primitive music. The savage sings what he can easily remember. Thus the Australian aborigine sings over and over again :—

(Quoted by Parry in *The Art of Music*)

And the English baby is beguiled with

Bye,   Ba - by   Bunt - ing.

which changes its words, but not its single fragment of tune through the whole nursery rhyme. The only alternative to endless repetition at this level is endless rhapsody, the formless chains of notes hummed under the breath unheeded, unremembered and unremarked. The rhapsodic principle finds a place sometimes in organized music in the shape of a cadenza by the soloist in a concerto, or in a moment of exuberance where a mere cascade of sound is desired. The fragments of aboriginal and nursery songs have already rhythmic organization by time and accent, which gives to the single phrase its unity. The next stage is to acquire contrast while still maintaining unity of idea; this is done as the Psalmist does it, by creating an anti-thetical phrase to balance the first, saying the same thing in different terms; this gives balance of phrase. Furthermore it is the beginning of a process of growth the logical outcome of which we can recognise in a fifty-minute long symphony of Elgar.

The next unifying factor is pattern. Melodic pattern is made by our old friends repetition and balance of phrase acting in conjunction. Having found a satisfactory bit of tune the singer gratifies the impulses both to repeat and to balance his phrases by singing it again. Grown more enterprising he is ready for a change and adds a new strain of melody. This too he must balance, but he will get lost and his tune will tumble to bits if he adds any more new material, so he repeats his first phrase by way of conclusion. This gives him the enormous satisfaction of recapitulation, of achieving unity in diversity and of making a further antithesis by means of his fourth phrase. The formula for this kind of tune, the commonest of all song tunes, is AA‖BA or A : ‖ BA, and its standard length is sixteen bars, made up of four four-bar phrases. This basic pattern, consisting essentially of four phrases of equal length made up of two different bits of material, is with the usual perversity of musical terminology called, not binary, but ternary form. The justification for it is not in the length or the disposition of the phrases in the tune, but in the logic of a tripartite division into statement—contrast—restatement. This ternary form is primarily a song form and belongs to vocal music ; it fits the emotional scheme of a common form of quatrain where, after an opening statement (line 1) and an amplification of it (line 2), something happens or the excitement rises in line 3, and line 4 sees the resolution. Applied to instrumental music—vocal and instrumental have always kept contra-accounts against each other—the scheme yields the same psychological satisfaction whether there are any words to make it explicit or not.

But beside voices we have two legs and require music for their exercise in the dance. Here what we need is a strain for moving this way and another strain for moving back. To and fro we go and for this purpose a binary arrangement suits us best. We will repeat our phrases to secure the pleasures of repetition and balance, but we will arrange them AA‖BB, or using the musical convention, A : ‖ : B. The essence of this binary form is antithesis and balance. We have therefore a binary and a ternary idea for application to musical architecture. In their simplest form of sixteen bars they are identical in length. For the reason that each divided neatly in half in the middle, instrumental pieces cast in song form were for a long time called binary and it is noteworthy that the repeat marks, the two dots :, survived at the end of an exposition of a symphony until after Brahms. Conductors do not nowadays always observe them, however.

The ternary idea was destined to predominate over the unitary (fugal) and the binary (dance) types of composition because its structural scheme could be reinforced by a further principle of design, namely modulation or a change of key, to call attention to the new material or to the change in the emotional temperature in the B section of a simple song. Thus the " Blue Bell of Scotland " is a perfect example of an orthodox tune in ternary form modulating to the dominant[1] key in the B section at the dramatic third line, " He's gone to fight the foe ".

This further principle of key, whose potentialities were first perceived in the seventeenth century, opened up vast possibilities of extended composition without endangering its unity. Key is a development from scale. It need hardly be said that people, least of all primitive people, do not think of a scale before they begin to sing and then sing in it. On the contrary, they sing a tune that expresses their feelings, but it is open to anyone who hears and can remember it to examine its melodic organization. Every tune is an orderly arrangement of tones, and if the constituent tones of a tune are set out in a scale the theorist, who is thus cold-bloodedly examining a *cri de coeur*, will observe what tones are selected and what are their inner relationships to each other.

Tunes derive their emotional character largely from the arrangement of the tones, semitones, microtones, or gaps of which they are composed. If the third degree of the scale is sharp it gives a certain emotional quality to the tune in which it occurs and we call it major ; if the third degree is flat, the emotional effect is quite different and we call it minor. The various forms of pentatonic mode, the Church modes with the Greek names and the familiar major and minor modes are such ways of internally organizing melodies. In the course of the last four centuries the major and minor scales have developed an elaborate system of harmony, which is nothing less than a

---

[1] The dominant is situate at the interval of a fifth above or a fourth below its tonic, and it is second only to the tonic in the strength of its influence in determining key.

plotting-out of the way to get about in what I may call tonal space, *i.e.* the orbit of our musical experience.

A chart of this self-contained tonal universe can be made by substituting letters for figures on a clock face in which all the twelve major keys can be set out, the sharps from 12 to 6, and the flats from 6 to 12 speaking clockwise. This gives a fair pictorial representation of the key system and enables the layman to get an idea of what is meant by modulation. Modulation means changing one's key, one's tonic,

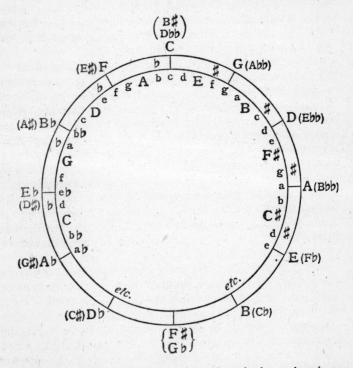

The hours marked on the outer circle are the major keys; the minutes are the tones and semitones of the scale. The capital letters on the inner circle are the relative minor keys with the same denomination of sharps and flats as their relative majors.

The purpose of the diagram is to represent the idea of tonal distance. It is for instance a long way from C minor to C sharp minor whereas G major is very near to D major, since there is a difference of only one degree of sharpness between them.

one's tonal centre. Furthermore the rather more difficult notion of a balance of keys can be envisaged. If starting from one's chosen tonic, say four o'clock on the dial, one modulates forwards *i.e.* in the clock-wise direction this will create a disturbance which can only be fully allayed by a temporary modulating in the reverse direction. More sharps are offset by a reduction in sharps, equilibrium is restored on returning to the home tonic at four o'clock. The ear (*i.e.* the mind in its tonal functioning) demands this equilibrium, and in experiencing first the disturbance, then the counter-disturbance and then the equilibrium, it has discovered the important artistic principles of change in identity, variety in unity, contrast and repetition.

This was the position reached in the time of Bach who wrote his *Well-Tempered Clavier*, containing the 48 Preludes and Fugues, two each in all twelve major and minor keys, to show that you can play round the circle, and those who like a game of clock golf can play one on their own piano in a short Prelude by Beethoven (Op 39, No. 2) which circles through all the sharp and flat keys from C to C round the dial. Later composers amused themselves and their audiences by crossing the circle by ingeniously varied routes, some by gradual and circuitous modulations, some by pivoting on a single chord or even a single note, and in the case of some modern composers by simply jumping. Holst, for instance, in his setting of the great Easter tune, " Lasst uns erfreuen ", to a paraphrase of Psalm CXLVIII, delights in jumping forwards and backwards from C to E, and in the *Hymn of Jesus* he keeps the same two keys fretting against one another without any padding of modulation for long tracts of the work.

In the seventeenth century instruments set about their emancipation from voices in earnest. They were no longer content to play variations on popular songs of the day or to write fantasias (of a fugal character) on scraps of plainsong, as the sixteenth century had been. The process can be seen clearly in the history of English music ; for the later developments we are bound to go to Germany. But in the seventeenth century English people were dancing mad and they even spread the contagion to the court of Louis XIV and so to the rest of civilized Europe. English dance tunes show how the binary and ternary ideas began to fertilize each other.

Examine the country-dance tunes in Playford's *The Dancing Master* (1650) and you find them binary structures in two sections, both in the same key with no halfway modulation. 'Argeers' has two well-defined parts with a double bar between them. 'Nonesuch' is similar in length, but its second part is derived thematically from the first and is therefore a less adventurous, possibly an earlier, as it is certainly a more rudimentary and tightly organized, tune. When French dances came in with James II we find Purcell writing minuets—very small and elementary minuets, which sometimes modulate in the middle and sometimes do not. In these binary dances it is common for the B music (*i.e.* the second section) to be repeated to provide more music for dance figures—this is found in a folk dance of the previous century like " Sellenger's Round ". In this way the second part gradually became longer ; in the classical minuet it is twice as long as the first part.

We find in Purcell the practice of grouping short dances together into Suites all in the same key. By the time of Handel the constituent dances of the suite are longer and their internal range of key wider. The binary form is still employed for them with a decisive modulation to the dominant at the end of the first part and a more leisurely return to the home key through other related keys in the second part, which is now decidedly longer than the first part. This became the established binary form of the eighteenth century and one can see it at its fullest development in Scarlatti's harpsichord sonatas.

But now the ternary idea began to make itself felt because the new material after the double bar was in a contrasting key, and, whatever the length and the pattern might determine, the key scheme was ABA, first key—secondary tonal centre—return to home key. The binary and ternary ideas combine even more clearly when to the minuet was added a second and generally shorter minuet called a trio (an unfortunate term whose justification is to be found not in logic but in history). After the trio the main minuet is repeated, a clear case of ABA in which both A and B are themselves binary structures. The minuet and trio alone of the dance forms of the suite survived into the symphony. Even so the latter part of the eighteenth century began to tire of it. Haydn is reported to have said that a new kind of minuet was needed. Beethoven made the required change by substituting a livelier scherzo for the decorous minuet but he kept the binary-ternary form of the minuet and trio for it.

The union of the binary and ternary ideas, however, produced a far more important offspring than the minuet and trio in sonata form itself. At some time between Bach and Haydn, unobtrusively in the middle years of the eighteenth century, this, the most fertile principle in all music, was conceived and quickly established itself as the dominant influence in musical composition. From that day to this it has provided composers with an architectural plan of apparently unlimited variety, flexibility and resource for the utterance of their thoughts, small as well as great, but mostly great. For it is essentially the vehicle for extended composition and substantial ideas. Its actual crystallization is attributed to Bach's son, Carl Philipp Emanuel; it first functioned freely and smoothly in Haydn; it was added to and enlarged by Beethoven; it has been modified in use by modern composers like Elgar, Bax, Vaughan Williams; it has only been thrown overboard for symphonic writing by Sibelius.

What then is this sonata form? It is a tripartite scheme of Exposition, Development and Recapitulation, in which the main principle of ternary form is secured by the Recapitulation (often in full) of the main material of the movement as set out in the Exposition. The Exposition itself keeps the old outlines of binary form in that it is concerned to state two groups of ideas in contrasted keys. So strong is the drag of history that First Subject and Second Subject persist as the names of these component sections though as a description they have long ceased to be accurate and are now positively misleading. By ' subject' is commonly understood a tune or a fairly concise theme such as the subject of a fugue. The second subject of a symphonic movement is nothing of the sort; it may consist of three or four distinct sections each with a musical idea of its own not necessarily in the same key. It comprises in fact all the material which the composer wishes to organize round his secondary key centre. One feature is commonly retained that does something to justify the misnomer 'second subject'; here probably, if anywhere, will be found a lyrical melody. A first subject is mainly concerned to establish the main key, a characteristic rhythm, and, maybe, a significant figure that is to run like a unifying thread right through the work. So that unless the composer is an incurable melodist like Schubert, there will be no appropriate place in it where its propulsive energy may relax and allow a more leisurely tune to emerge. The place for this feminine element therefore is in the second subject.

Male and female created He them—the principle runs through all creation—and sonata form has often been compared to a drama in which the first subject represents the dynamic male, the second the more tender (and often more loquacious) heroine, the Development section the working out of their destiny and the Recapitulation the resolution of the conflict, and by the implication of the identity of key that is therein established, the reconciliation of the principal persons of the drama. This dramatic way of regarding the least theatrical form of music, though too circumscribed, is in the main justifiable at any rate as applied to classical German symphonies, for conflict is of the essence of drama, (as the Greeks long ago showed by calling an actor ἀγωνιστής, a contestant), and a symphonic movement is a highly concentrated if impersonal conflict of ideas which are ultimately shown to be congruent. At any rate symphony and drama both conform to one of the human mind's fundamental ways of seeking the truth—to set two forces in antithesis and then resolve their conflict. Drama differs from symphony in that it may reach its conclusion through catastrophe and the elimination of one of the contesting forces ; symphony never wholly eliminates the participatory forces but always reaches equilibrium—a fact which is due to the peculiar properties conferred on it by the balance of keys.

A quotation or two from familiar symphonies may give point to these generalizations.

Consider how Mozart in the " Jupiter " symphony, Beethoven in the C minor symphony and Brahms in his third symphony set over against a dynamic first subject a glowing tuneful section in their second subject.

Mozart begins eruptively with

but includes in his second subject the formally patterned and graceful little tune

Beethoven begins even more abruptly with

which dominates the whole movement, but cannot wholly suppress a milder argument in the relative major and relatively mild key of E flat

Brahms launches himself *passionato* on a swinging arpeggio

but makes a complete break at his second subject, changing his rhythm from duple to triple and his mood from *passionato* to *grazioso*

These quotations are not representative but rather indicative of the potentialities of the form and of a natural tendency to use it in a certain way. Indeed generalizations about sonata form are more unsafe and more liable to be riddled with reservations and exceptions than those of any other department of organized knowledge I can think of. They are comparable perhaps to the irregular verbs of a foreign language, for whose irrational behaviour the ultimate justification is only seen in the light of wide philological principles and an intimate acquaintance with the genius of the particular language concerned. Any symphony can be analysed along the main lines of sonata form ; no symphony whatever corresponds to the formula which is the best available synopsis of the principles involved. And it cannot be too strongly or too frequently asserted that sonata form is not an engineer's blue print by use of which composers can run off masterpieces. Themes have a life of their own and are not so many rods and pulleys that can be built into any machine ready-made. Sonata form in fact is an organic principle, not a craftsman's pattern ; it is not even an architect's standard ground-plan for a particular type of building, like a church, though its general lay-out is constant ; it might more properly be compared with the form of a tree. Trees differ from each other in species, shape, size, according to their kind, locality, position, so that no two are alike, but all trees have roots, trunks, branches and leaves. So, then , most symphonies have a skeletal structure which can be tabulated as follows :

EXPOSITION	DEVELOPMENT	RECAPITULATION
First subject or group of ideas in the main key	In which these subjects are discussed.	First subject repeated in the tonic key ; the link is adjusted to bring back the second subject also in the tonic.
Link		
Second subject or group of subjects in secondary key or keys.		

The text books are inclined to leave the matter at this point and say of the development that therein the composer pleases himself ; some of them even call it a free fantasia. This is to succumb to the blue-print view of sonata form. In the development section the composer not only ' develops ' (in the technical sense of breaking up, elongating, re-assembling, and treating in imitation the themes that have already been stated) but he adjusts the relative lengths of the two subjects, manipulates the balance of keys, sometimes inserts an alien episode in order to secure a new point of contrast, and does everything which his skill as a composer suggests to extract further implications from

his subject-matter, sometimes showing in the process an underlying, but not immediately obvious, relationship between his
two subjects.   The first movement of Beethoven's fourth symphony in B flat provides a good example of what a development
is for and what, musically speaking, it can do.   It is a matter of
great difficulty to describe musical events in words even when
the use of technical terms and musical illustrations is granted.
Here however is an attempt to indicate the play and balance of
forces in a symphonic movement.

After a somewhat mysterious slow introduction the first
movement proper bursts away in high spirits with a flourish
and a pert little tune founded on an arpeggio—

(*a*) is the flourish, (*b*) the pert tune, and (*c*) are smiling chords of
the sixth which round it off.   This is really all the material
of the first subject, though there are some syncopations in the
bridge passage that leads to the second subject.   Syncopations
are a feature of this symphony and they here suggest an eager-
ness to push on to the second subject which begins without ado
in the dominant key, *i.e.* F major, with another perky tune ;

(*d*) *Bassoon*

which is tossed about in dialogue among the wind instruments.

A strange passage of minims in sequence follows:

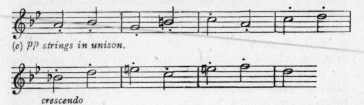

(e) *pp strings in unison.*

crescendo

For all its open-hearted gaiety and general happiness there is in this symphony an undercurrent of mystery first sounded in the Introduction, alluded to here, and recrudescent in the Development. However, an untroubled lyrical tune restores a placid mood of confidence.

(f) *clarinet*

The rest of the exposition is taken up with assertions of the tonality of F in contrasting bursts of loud and soft tone and the syncopations already mentioned. In sum this second subject runs to about 90 bars, or deducting bridge passage and final codetta (the syncopations) at least seventy bars, as against the forty-five of the first subject. This disproportion is compensated in the Development where (a) and (b) of the first subject hold the floor for forty bars in keys on the sharp side of the main key. Then a new tune appears in the even sharper key of G :—

It is new, though it sounds so natural as almost to escape notice. It is repeated five times swinging back the tonality, as it goes, to a point further on the flat side of B flat, namely E flat. There is an abrupt jump back to (a) again as the whole orchestra picks up once more the substance of (a) and (b), but after pivoting on an ambiguous chord the harmony shifts by an enharmonic change far over into the sharp keys to B major, *i.e.* the tonality (or key feeling) moves over seven degrees of sharpness right across to the other side of the circle, but it extricates itself by a chromatic drop of a semitone into B flat. The drum (very important in this symphony) ensures that no further divagations are permitted by rolling continuously on the tonic B flat and the Recapitulation follows. In all this (amounting to 150 bars) there has been no reference to the second subject, which however is duly recapitulated in full and adds its voice in support of the main tonality of B flat. The coda of thirty bars leaves the second subject alone and concentrates on (*a*) and (*c*).

If the reader has been able to picture what has thus painfully been described he will have before him no neatly symmetrical construction run off from the sonata blue-print, but a vision of a high-spirited theme *a*, *b*, and *c*, running off with a movement in spite of three different types of argument *d*, *e*, and *f* brought against it at greater length. The mood of the development, however, imposes a check, which is to say that the first subject itself contains the elements that will balance up its own exuberance, and the battle of keys ensures that, though the more vigorous theme (the dashing hero) triumphs, a satisfactory equilibrium is reached.

In the matter of keys the balance may be further adjusted by the sequence of keys of the remaining movements of the symphony. The ' Emperor ' piano concerto provides an example of a swerve towards the flats which is made in the opening bars by a plunge to the subdominant[1] chord, being retrieved in the middle section by a deliberate migration to the sharps, so as to bring the mind back to the tonic at the end of the movement, but still necessitating in the second movement a key signature of five sharps to offset the excessive flatness of the tonality of E flat in the first movement.

In the matter of structure the skeleton of sonata form had two optional appendages from its earliest use by Haydn, a slow introduction and a coda (or tailpiece). Mozart normally dispensed with an introduction and plunged *in medias res*. Of his forty-nine symphonies only four have this feature which had

---

[1] The subdominant is a fourth above or a fifth below the tonic and has a tendency to lead the ear towards the flat side of the key in contrast to the dominant whose bias is towards sharps.

previously been found in the French Overture, whereas Haydn prefaces thirty-five of his hundred and four symphonies with a weighty prelude.[1] Of Beethoven's nine symphonies Nos. 1, 2, 4 and 7 have introductions of considerable substance and power, charged with something more than a summons to attention. Similarly and even more so Beethoven enlarged and deepened the coda, which became a kind of second development section (in Nos. 3 and 5 for instance) of equal length to the middle of the movement. This made room for further possibilities of adjusting the balance of keys and the prominence of thematic material. A wider choice and freer use of keys consequently became possible. A later stage was reached when a composer did not state his themes and reserve all his ingenuity for the development section but more gradually unfolded his purpose. A germinal motif (such as Beethoven had used in the Fifth Symphony) might be enunciated and then elaborated at once. The logical extremity of this process is reached by Walton in his symphony where his themes hardly ever appear twice alike, but are recognisable because all the forms obviously derive from a common origin.

Sibelius often presents one with the irreducible core of a theme and then evolves the complete theme for subsequent presentation in full. This process of developing a theme from a motif is the inverse of classical development, which normally worked by breaking up the theme into constituent phrases, restating them in augmentation, diminution, inversion or whatever. The modern way is to hammer motifs into themes. An extension of this process can be seen in the Epilogue which is a structural feature employed by Vaughan Williams and Bax; at the very end of the symphony a passage occurs summarizing, as it were, all that has been previously discussed and often revealing in the conclusions so drawn a fundamental relationship between the themes that hitherto were differentiated. Bax's fifth symphony ends with a broad chorale-like tune whose purpose is just precisely to prove the inter-relationship of all the thematic material of the symphony.

Sonata form, as here described, is almost invariably employed for the first movements of symphonies. The scherzo follows the minuet and trio pattern. The slow movement may be in simple ternary form like a song—it may even be a march, as in the Eroica—or it will more likely be in sonata form adapted

[1] See Appendix II.

to more lyrical thematic material by curtailing its development.
The finale may be a set of variations—also a possibility for a
slow movement—or a rondo, especially the developed rondo
mostly employed by Beethoven. Concertos follow the same
general architectural principles as symphonies, sonatas and
chamber music, but in a concerto a place has to be found for
the virtuosity of the soloist.

Two important later developments were to emerge in the
middle of the nineteenth century, each of them an attempt at
a greater organic unity. There is a certain emotional congruity
between the movements of a symphony and attention is paid
to the distribution of keys so that the work as a whole shall
achieve variety of key and yet present a balance of tonality at
the end of the finale. But it was possible for Beethoven to
substitute an entirely different movement for one already
written. He discarded the Andante Favori as unsuitable for
the 'Waldstein' sonata and he was prevailed upon to write a new
finale for the late quartet in B flat in place of the Grosse Fuge.
Schubert on the other hand, prolific as he was, was stumped
by the problem of finding the right movement for continuing
the 'Unfinished Symphony'. The problem of binding the
constituent movements of a sonata or symphony into a closer
unity was therefore a natural one to arise. The two proposed
solutions are associated in the first instance with the names of
Liszt and Franck. Liszt's method was to condense into a
single movement the distinct moods of the usual four movements. This single-movement form he applied to his piano
sonata, and it has been a good deal employed in recent times
in chamber music, where it took to itself the unsuitable name of
Phantasy. The principle of amalgamating diverse self-subsistent
sections into a single movement has been used for orchestral
works, but there is no conspicuous instance of a symphony laid
out on a symphonic scale in Liszt's condensed sonata form,
until we come to Sibelius who does something of the sort in
his seventh symphony.

But unification by the other method—the use of themes
common to several movements—has been tried fairly widely.
The most thorough-going instance is Debussy's string quartet
where the same theme, differently spelt, serves three of the four
movements. But in orchestral music Franck's symphony is
the most conspicuous of the new 'cyclic' form. Franck

gathers together themes from his preceding movements and quotes them in the finale. Beethoven had done the same in the Choral Symphony, where he passed in review the principal themes of the earlier movements only to reject them ; his purpose was in fact purely dramatic. Franck's intention was to weld the whole together by this revised form of recapitulation. Quotation however is not true recapitulation, and though Debussy's quartet is brilliantly successful, it may be doubted whether thematic repetition necessarily increases the organic unity of a work, and it may even disrupt the finale. The modern method of the epilogue, in which the thematic material of the whole work is shown to have a basic connexion which is not made explicit until it has all been heard and developed, is probably a better solution of this problem. Symphonies continue to be written in which the organic connexion resides in the composer's mind and the general emotional complexion of the work is not made explicit by any technical feature. But we are sometimes reminded of the persistence of this problem of artistic creation, which is peculiar to music, by such a circumstance as Walton's failure to find a finale for his symphony till some time after the other movements had been completed, performed and seen to belong together.

CHAPTER VI

THE SYMPHONY

THE symphony today holds pride of place in music. It may be that operas, oratorios and other works involving voices embrace a wider span of human emotion and may therefore be accounted greater works of art, but the symphony represents the highest point of evolution reached by the art of music : it is self-contained and unfettered, at once subtle and powerful, and stands at the furthest point where the human spirit with its feet firmly grounded on the reality of experience looks out to the infinite where there are no more than inklings, hints and shadowy possibilities of what lies behind mortal knowledge. Philosophers from Plato to Samuel Alexander, when they have been sensitive at all to æsthetic experience, have conceded that music has some such metaphysical affinity with the ultimate roots of things, even while regarding its detachment from other modes of thought and feeling as one of its most important and distinctive characteristics. Architecture is earthbound, painting is tied to the visible shapes of the physical world, poetry is only half articulate, but music can soar clean out of the world and carry the human spirit with it into a realm of rarified and subtilized experience that gives us some of our strongest intimations of immortality.

Yet if one had said this to old Father Haydn, he would no doubt have shaken his head and said that when writing his 104 symphonies he did not dwell on these mountain tops ; he was content to satisfy his princely employer and give to God the glory and thanks for his talent. He did give to God glory and thanks : ' I know ', he said, ' that God has bestowed a talent on me, and I thank Him for it '. But he was not solemn about the products of his genius. Of his own works he said " Sunt mala mixta bonis " (There are bad mixed with the good); " some of my children are well-bred, some ill-bred and here and there is a changeling among them ". There was no special sanctity about the word symphony. By derivation it means no more than voices in association (Greek σύν = with or together, φωνη=a voice) and seventeenth century composers applied it to any little instrumental prelude or interlude, but more particularly to the introductions to operas. Even then however the ' voice ' had ceased to mean a human voice and meant a contrapuntal voice, a ' part ' for an instrument, not a throat, to sing. To this day the word can be used without gross error in commercial music for four bars of instrumental vamping ' till ready ' for the voice to enter. But during the early and middle parts of the eighteenth century it was used along with Divertimento, Cassation, Serenade, for independent instrumental compositions. When Haydn came to establish the symphony on its proper foundations he did without doubt attach a certain dignity to the meaning of the word. What, however, shows that it carries exalted connotations and should not be cheaply used is the increasing restraint shown by composers in symphonic writing. Haydn wrote over a hundred symphonies, Mozart, prolific as he was, barely fifty, Beethoven was content with the immortal nine, Brahms, waiting till full maturity and middle life before he embarked on a symphony at all, said his say in four. The Slav composers, who are not so prone to the reverential solemnity of the Germans, are still not prodigal with symphonies. Dvorak wrote nine, and Tchaikovsky six, of which they both allowed their early essays to sink into obscurity. Berlioz and Franck, representing the French tradition, wrote only one each. Sibelius, most acclaimed of modern symphonists and with justice, has concentrated the highest thoughts of a fertile mind—and what concentration!—into seven symphonies. The composer is only playing fair with his public if he takes the composition of a symphony very seriously. When we attend to a symphony we ask to have our minds deeply engaged, whether the subject happens to be grave or gay, tragic or genial ; we ask for logic as well as feeling, order as well as impulse, and some sort of catharsis by discipline.

The symphony in several movements evolved out of the ' Sinfonia avanti l' opera ', the instrumental prelude to opera (or oratorio) to which the word was originally applied, through the Italian Overture. When dramatic music captivated Italy and France in the seventeenth century, composers soon began to elaborate their preludes in order to give weight to the entertainment that was to follow and call the attention of the audience to the importance and imposing scale of the new form of art. In France Lully employed what came to be known as the French Overture, *i.e.* a short, broad and slow introduction followed by a quick fugal movement and sometimes rounded off with a minuet or other dance movement. Handel's overtures are of this type. But the Italians arrange their contrasting movements the other way round : the Italian Overture begins with a substantial allegro movement, followed by an expressive slow movement and concluded with a lighter quick movement, often in some form of triple measure to offset the square time of the opening allegro. It was from this type of overture, which had firmly established itself by the beginning of the eighteenth century, that the symphonies which Mozart heard and admired so much at Mannheim were derived.

We do not hear much of the Mannheim school (whose chief names are those of the Stamitz family and F. Xavier Richter) in our concert halls, nor of the two Bachs, Emanuel and Christian, who did much to crystallize symphonic form into the shape adopted and developed by Haydn. When we do, we are apt to give them scant justice, since we listen to them with unhistorical ears. If this is unfair there is this excuse, that in the recent reaction from nineteenth century fashions and tastes we have plunged headlong into the eighteenth century and given ourselves a surfeit of these early symphonies and concertos. We then begin to observe that idioms which we thought were personal to Mozart are the commonplaces of his period and, wearying of eighteenth century formulæ, we react in the characteristic British fashion and say that none but the best is good enough for us. Critical and historical listening is the best line of approach to this transitional music of the eighteenth century.

Perhaps the chief contribution of these transitional composers to the symphony was a more flexible style of performance and a willingness to explore a wider range of sentiment. The Mannheim crescendo was famous and was part of the tendency which substituted a flexible gradation of power for the old alternation of loud and soft in antithetical but unequal masses. Bach's sons did not restrict themselves to the restraint and dignity of their father but wrote in the ' galant ' style, *i.e.* in a lighter vein which aimed at pleasing by flirting with more irresponsible sentiments.

HAYDN'S SYMPHONIES

Haydn's long career (1732–1809) was not too long for so great a task as the establishment of the string quartet and the orchestral symphony. The circumstances of his life were favourable for this historic mission. His first appointment at the age of twenty-three was at a gentleman's country house near Melk, where he had at his disposal a few strings and a couple each of oboes and horns. Here at Weinzirl he produced his first quartet and his first symphony, both containing minuets in addition to movements adapted from Emanuel Bach's model of the sonata. In 1761 he took service with Prince Esterhazy and remained in that noble household till 1790. During those thirty years he had ample opportunity for experiment. He was much liked not only by his employer but by the musicians on the establishment. For most of the time the Prince resided at his new palace in Hungary which was remote from the world of Vienna. The result was that Haydn did an enormous amount of uninterrupted work. He explained the situation thus : " As a conductor of an orchestra I could make experiments, observe what produced an effect and what weakened it, and was thus in a position to improve, alter, make additions or omissions and be as bold as I pleased ; I was cut off from the world, there was no one to confuse and torment me, and I was forced to become original ". Original he is. Never does he write a quartet or symphony but somewhere in it he shakes some surprise out of his sleeve. This indeed is the chief distinction between his and Mozart's use of the courtly language of the eighteenth century. Mozart's movements are regular and perfectly mannered, which is not to say that they are written to formula. But one cannot picture Mozart letting out the *Paukenschlag*, the sudden onslaught of horn, trumpet and drum at the end of a mincing little staccato phrase of a sedate slow movement, as Haydn does in the ' Surprise ' symphony. Nor of his contriving anything so naively charming as to allow a finale to run down into quiet two-part counterpoint as a hint to an employer that the musicians wanted to leave their isolation at Esterhaz and go home to family and holiday in Vienna, as Haydn did in the ' Farewell ' symphony, in which one after another the players blow out their candles and leave their desks till only two violins are left. Even the solo drum

roll which begins the E flat symphony (hence nicknamed
'*Paukenwirbel*' or '*Drumroll*') is a mild eccentricity, very
characteristic of Haydn's straightforward yet original mind,
which always has some happy and unexpected turn of phrase
to enliven his most orderly proceedings.

After Prince Esterhazy's death Haydn lived another nineteen years in which he showed the freshness of his mind on a
larger scale by producing an entirely new kind of work, his
oratorio *The Creation*.   This was one product of his two visits
to London, whither he went at the invitation of the impresario,
Johann Salomon, in 1791 immediately he was free from the
Esterhazy service.   For this visit he composed six symphonies
and for a second visit in 1794-5, following the enormous success
of the first, he composed six more.   These twelve London
symphonies are his greatest works in this form and stand apart
from the rest.   In them all the experience of years came to
fruition and in their mastery may be detected the stimulus
which he had received from Mozart.   Between 1781 and 1791
he and Mozart met at intervals, were continuously on good
terms with one another and influenced each other powerfully.
The essential feature of these later symphonies was the expan-
sion of the development section of the movement.   He had
discovered the essence of it, the principle of 'working out' the
implications of the themes, in some quartets which he published
in 1781 and described as being composed in an entirely new
style.   A favourite way of beginning these expanded development sections is to put a theme or part of a theme contrapuntally in imitation against itself—as can be seen in the ' Oxford '
and ' Drumroll ' symphonies.   Another favoured device is to
set it out in sharp relief on the wind instruments alone, as in
the D major symphony, No. 7 of the London set.   This symphony provides a good example of another and more general
characteristic, his affinity with Beethoven—Beethoven is much
more Haydn's child than Mozart's.   The arresting introduction
in the sombre key of D minor leads into an allegro movement
based on one of those diatonic tunes such as Beethoven used
to make out of contiguous notes of the scale, but the gait of the
movement is lighter than Beethoven would have made it.
The finale of this symphony is cast on big lines in sonata form
with an important development (started contrapuntally) and,
though its main tune is jolly and animated, as befits a finale,

the second subject contains a short section of a more reserved, not to say mysterious, character, which is expanded during the development. Here again is a Beethovenian movement—with a hint of the Pastoral Symphony to come, but nimbler, more smiling in its humour, less rough and ' unbuttoned ' than Beethoven. For his slow movements Hadyn was fond of variations, and where the movement is not divided formally into sections, he likes to linger over and repeat his melodies with arabesques and embellishments. He standardized the minuet as a regular feature of the symphony, making four the normal number of movements. But the writing of so many minuets in quartet, sonata and symphony seems to have taxed even his fertile imagination, or at any rate to have produced a too stereotyped effect, since he is said to have remarked that it was time someone found a new kind of minuet, as he had found out how to write a new kind of first movement. Beethoven was to meet his requirements by producing the scherzo.

MOZART'S SYMPHONIES

Mozart began writing symphonies when he was eight, and his first two were written in Chelsea, where he was staying with his father while on his prodigy tour. They are in the style of John Christian Bach, then at the height of his fame in London and organizer of the concerts at which the boy Mozart appeared. Only seven of the forty-eight, a total which includes one or two that he used as opera overtures, call for any extended comment, though occasionally an early symphony like one in A (K201), that dates from 1774, is instructive in showing how sonata form was developing in Mozart's hands as compared with its contemporary development in Haydn's. This particular symphony in A, written at Salzburg when the composer was eighteen, is itself a charming work and marks his emergence from immaturity. But its structure belongs to the old order. Three of its four movements are constructed on the binary principle—the fourth is an orthodox minuet and trio. The double bar occurs nearly half way through and each section is marked to be repeated ; there is little development and the second section is not much more than a looser and lengthier re-statement of the material of the first section ; the first subject, in the first movement a sequence based on a falling octave and a rising appogiatura, predominates, as usual in the days before the full emergence of sonata form. There is however a coda.

The " Paris " symphony (K 297), written four years later, shows a marked change to the later type of sonata form with exposition of two contrasted subjects, adequate development and recapitulation, and it is scored for the full orchestra of the day, including clarinets, which was available for the Concert Spirituel. Mozart wrote of it to his father that the promoters of the Paris concerts were very pleased with it. " I am myself quite satisfied with it", he continued, " whether it will please generally I do not know ; and truth to say I care very little ; for whom have I to please ? The very few intellectual Frenchmen that there are I can answer for ; as for the stupid ones, it does not signify much whether they are pleased or not. But I am in hopes that even the donkeys will find something to admire. I have not omitted the *premier coup d'archet* and that is enough for them. What a fuss they make about it, to be sure ! *Was Teufel* ! I see no difference ; they just begin together, as they do elsewhere ; it is quite ludicrous ! "

The *premier coup d'archet* means the attack by a full orchestra. Mozart did however see a difference, for he deliberately refrained from beginning his finale so and substituted an opening in which the violins played a duet of eight bars before there was a tutti. One other feature of this brilliant symphony is that he wrote two slow movements for it. French taste liked its music short, and at the impresario's suggestion Mozart wrote a curtailed andante and for the same reason omitted the minuet.

The ' Haffner ' symphony, originally planned as a serenade for some festivity in the house of the burgomaster of Salzburg, reverts however to an earlier manner of instrumental composition, the unitary or monothematic form used by Bach in his concertos, though the orchestral lay-out is in the later fashion. The whole of the first movement is again built on an unmelodious theme of leaping octaves. In the last movement is a self-quotation : Osmin's song of premature triumph in *Die Entführung* provides the theme of the first episode. Pleased with this touch, Mozart recalls it and so anticipates the practice by which Beethoven converted the simple rondo into the more extended sonata-rondo.

The ' Linz ' symphony (K 425), so called because it was

dedicated to Mozart's friend and benefactor Count Thun who lived at Linz, where the symphony had its first performance, belongs to the same year, 1783. It has a slow introduction, which leads to a brilliant first movement in C major. Trumpets, horns and drums were available at Linz but not flutes or clarinets ; the trumpets and drums are even retained for a tender slow movement ; the two wood-wind instruments have their fun in the trio of the minuet. If the thematic material of this movement is examined—it can be taken as typical mature Mozart—it will be observed that there is very little melody in it. Mozart was not an instinctive melodist like Schubert, or even like Haydn, though of course words and dramatic situations in the operas elicited some immortal melody of the formal, sustained and extended kind. But the genius of Mozart consists in transmuting common formulæ, rhythmic marchings and countermarchings, arpeggios, runs, five-finger exercises, little figures of repeated notes, and (especially) feminine cadences, into a texture of such exquisite sweetness as to give the illusion of a lyricism which it does not in thematic fact possess.

The next symphony is a bigger thing, though it is in only three movements and lacks a minuet. It was first performed at Prague during Mozart's successful visit to that city to superintend *Figaro* and it is consequently known as the ' Prague ' symphony (K 504). It also begins with a grave introduction and all three movements are in sonata form, which is elastic enough to admit a closely worked first movement, a gentle and decorated andante and a finale tumbling over itself in its haste. Its content is of a weight to form a fitting prelude to the last three great symphonies composed in a single year (1788). These are the E flat (K 543), the G minor (K 550) and the " Jupiter " in C major (K 551), each a work of supreme achievement on any computation whatsoever.

Mozart's distinctive contribution to instrumental music was his renovation of the concerto. That, historically speaking, is his importance outside the sphere of opera. But music is more than its own history, and the three great symphonies, utterly unlike each other although products of the same mind at the same moment of its development and written, incidentally, at a time of trouble when the shadows were beginning to close in upon him, are works of art outside time.

The E flat (K 543) is a passionate and dramatic work that

constantly suggests *Don Giovanni*. Sometimes in the development sections one is almost deceived into thinking oneself in the middle of a great operatic ensemble, and the illusion is strengthened by the sudden alternations of feeling and the momentary interjections of another mood, as though a character standing by has a point to make amid the onward drive of events. There is in all this drama, however, no suggestion of autobiography, whereas in the G minor symphony (K 550) one cannot escape the feeling that behind the exquisite manners and the regularity of form the strain of personal melancholy, which often found an outlet in this same key, colours the work. Perhaps this is why it is the best loved of all Mozart's symphonies, for while it does not, as Tchaikovsky does, magnify a private sorrow into a public lament but maintains the emotional distance proper to all classical art, the latent personal feeling in it strikes more immediately at the listener's heart than elsewhere in Mozart. It has been suggested that this " supreme achievement of eighteenth century instrumental music " (Hadow) which is to say a supremely classical work, is also the " sunrise of romanticism " (Blom). One cannot altogether reject the adjective romantic and one must therefore agree with the justice of Mr. Blom's conclusion that in this symphony " classicism and romanticism meet and once and for all we see a perfect equilibrium between them ".

There is however nothing romantic about the 'Jupiter' (K 551), and whoever coined the nickname perceived in it a certain Olympian serenity that lies beyond the drama and romance of the other two contemporary symphonies. The key is C major and in the finale a passage in fugue counterbalances the symphonic statement of a more than usually colourless theme. It is Mozart's alchemy that with a string of commonplace tags he creates a texture which somehow reconciles the divergent methods of fugue and sonata in an amazing piece of sheer musical construction. Here is to be found the summary of eighteenth-century classicism.

BEETHOVEN

Whereupon Beethoven came and upset it. Haydn's ' London' symphonies fill the gap of the seventeen-nineties. Promptly with the dawn of a new century Beethoven launched his conception of the symphony upon the world and he began as

he meant to go on. He struck a discord in F by way of
announcing that his key after a feint towards G was to be C,
and thereafter he began to upset the equilibrium of form and
matter, to admit a dynamic force which disrupted the conventions of Haydn and Mozart, and to fill the symphonic mould
so full that it finally burst and spilled itself over in the choral
finale of the Ninth Symphony. The chief overt formal change
was the substitution of a scherzo for a minuet. He did this
in the First Symphony though he did not openly avow it, as in
the Second Symphony, but retained the title minuet without
however retaining its sedate pace. In the Fourth and Seventh
Symphonies he repeats his trios and orders an additional
repetition of the minuet to correspond. In the Ninth Symphony his trio is in duple time. In the Eighth Symphony
he reverts to a true minuet—Wagner expatiates at length in
his essay 'On Conducting' on the iniquity of Mendelssohn and
other German conductors in missing the real character of this
movement by taking it too fast. But in general the emotional
balance of the symphony as a musical organism is changed to
something more robust and more vigorous by the substitution
of a scherzo, though the word itself merely means 'a joke'—
but then Beethoven's joke is like a slap on the back that nearly
knocks you down.

There is something Haydnish in the First Symphony, especially in the finale, and the Second Symphony may be regarded
superficially as Mozartian—though the forcefulness of Beethoven's mind shows itself in the dynamics. In the Third we
pass into new territory. It is in the first place much longer
than any symphony written up to that time (1804). In the
second place the disposition of the movements is unusual; its
enormous first movement is followed by a Funeral March and
its finale is a set of variations on a theme which Beethoven had
already used elsewhere and which had for him a special significance. But its most conspicuous difference is in the subject-
matter—big issues are raised and a hint as to their nature is
given in its dedication ' to the memory of a great man ' and in
its title ' Eroica '. The starting point for the symphony was no
doubt Napoleon and the libertarian politics of the day with which
Beethoven sympathized, but it is no external programme which
is illustrated here, it is rather the working out in music of
Beethoven's own problem. In the Fifth Symphony the struggle

issues in victory, in the Seventh Symphony his soul is set free and in the Ninth it reaches out to a larger communion of souls. The odd-numbered symphonies are admittedly bigger than the even, whether one accepts this ethico-psychological suggestion or not, and size in works of art is determined by subject-matter. The subject matter of the struggle—and struggle is unmistakable—is self-conquest. Despair came to Beethoven in the form of the threat of his deafness. He lost his hearing, but he conquered his despair, and the choice of his ' Prometheus ' theme as the subject of variations in the finale of the ' Eroica ' symbolized for him the idea of dauntless creation. In the Fifth Symphony the struggle is sharp but the issue from minor to major in the finale is decisive. Apart from the fact that trombones make their appearance at this point in his scores this movement is interesting in that it is linked to the scherzo and during its course reverts to the music of the scherzo. The Seventh Symphony was called by Wagner the apotheosis of the dance, and appropriately enough, since every movement is markedly rhythmic in character. More penetrating, though less often quoted, was his observation that in it we are brought into touch with the processes of Nature. Beethoven himself gave some colour to this interpretation in one of his chaotic attempts at verbal self-expression—" Almighty One in the woods I am blessed......Every tree speaks through thee ". And the overwhelming unity of the work, secured by a rhythm that persists through all contrasts of subjects, does suggest the irresistible urge of life revealing itself in the process of growth, as it may be seen in the life of a tree — the seed sprouting, the plant unfolding, the sap rising, and the fruit swelling in abundance. The clue to the Ninth Symphony is to hand in the words which Beethoven chose for his choral finale—Schiller's *Ode to Joy*—which hymns a universal brotherhood in which seraph and earth-worm join with humanity in praise of their Creator. Out of the brooding mystery of the first movement comes an exuberant scherzo and a slow movement of heart-easing melody, leading by a dramatic piece of instrumental dialogue to the entry of voices in an elaborate set of variations on one of the great diatonic melodies of the world.

The even numbered symphonies are cast in less heroic mould and depict the more gracious, more feminine side of things. Number 4 reflects a period of happiness in Beethoven's life.

No. 6, the Pastoral, is a thorough-going programme symphony complete with thunderstorm and bird-calls which question the accuracy of Beethoven's claim that it is more feeling than painting. No. 8, in the same key, F, is all good-humour. Interspersed between the more intense odd-numbered symphonies these lighter symphonies help to complete the emotional range which is the strength of the unique appeal that Beethoven's symphonies have made to all sorts and conditions of men of all nations in the hundred and more years since they have dominated the orchestral repertory.

SCHUBERT, SCHUMANN AND BRAHMS.

If the philosophical content of Beethoven's symphonies was humanistic and ethical—and Goethe, his contemporary, detected such a quality which had not hitherto been present in music without definite religious associations—that of Brahms is predominantly logical. Each of the four symphonies has a germinal motif that pervades its thought, most markedly in Nos. 2 and 3. No. 1 has a phrase of three rising semitones which appears in the very first bar ; No. 2 leads off with a four-note motif of level crotchets in the bass which is pursued into the finale through many other thematic relationships. No. 3 is concerned with the three notes F A F ; No. 4 has a falling third and a triad which develops from it. Then too the key relationships are interesting. The individual movements of No. 1 are in keys that mount by thirds—C minor, E major, A flat and C minor. No. 3, which is concerned from the start to pursue the relationship of A flat to F major, pursues also a sequence of keys which grow progressively darker—F major, C major, C minor, F minor. No. 4 goes from E minor to E major, introduced by a horn-call in C, C major follows and E minor returns for the finale. No. 4 has a further logical interest. Brahms's admirers were disturbed at its early performances because its finale is a Passacaglia, *i.e.* a movement constructed on the repetition of the same phrase of eight bars thirty times over, an abnormal ending for a symphony, and the movement is certainly a *tour de force*. But the first movement is half inclined to become a passacaglia itself, so persistent are the opening bars of the first subject, and so pervasive the falling thirds, and what seems to have been at the back of Brahms's mind through the symphony was the reconciliation of sonata form with variation form.

Brahms waited till he was forty-three before he gave to an expectant world his first symphony in C minor. His fourth and last was written in 1884–5. All came within a period of ten years from 1875, the first two close together and then the last two also close together, but after an interval of eight years. They are thus fully representative of his mind in maturity and they are strikingly different from one another. No. 1 is an epic, No. 2 more lyrical, No. 3 comes nearer to being a personal document, and No. 4 is more consciously detached and monumental like the 'Jupiter' of Mozart. There is a tendency in them all except No. 2 to throw the main weight into the last movement. No. 1 opens massively enough in storm and stress, and its leonine strength is balanced in the finale with an even longer movement that is constructed on a plan of unusual proportions, of which incidentally a very good description has been given by Mr. J. B. Priestley in his novel, *Angel Pavement*. A slow Introduction contains a medley of material; the tune known as the Cambridge quarters (though one of the bells anticipates its turn in a Scotch snap) is announced *passionato* by horn and flute, and then when the allegro arrives comes the great tune, whose cousinship with that in the Ninth Symphony led some of Brahms's admirers to call this C minor symphony "The Tenth". There is no development section; a second subject of fair dimensions leads straight in to the recapitulation, which however, is expanded to contain references to the Introduction. Between these two great movements are two gentle ones, a song-like andante in place of a scherzo, and an allegretto marked *grazioso*.

The second symphony in D is shorter and sunny throughout. Brahms even described it as a " set of waltzes " because two of its movements are in three-four time. Another *grazioso* movement is substituted for a scherzo but it is interrupted by *presto* episodes. In the first of these episodes the tune is the same, but the pace and the time and the rhythm are different; in the second the tune, if such it can be called, is new though possibly derived from the same stock. Brahms tried elsewhere, notably in the A major violin sonata, this mingling of slow movement with scherzo. Here the mixture is certainly successful. There is psychology as well as logic in the third symphony

in F, which perhaps offers the best text in all symphonic literature for a discourse on " the meaning of music ". Brahms as
a young man took as his motto ' frei aber froh ' (' free but
happy '), a re-writing of ' frei aber einsam ' (' free but lonely ').
From this motif F, A flat (or natural), F, Brahms proceeds
to develop an extended argument. He strikes a chord of F major,
including, that is, an A natural in the first bar, and follows it
with a conspicuous A flat in the next bar—a harmonic oxymoron
known as a ' false relation ', which was common enough in
early English counterpoint but rare in later German harmony.
In bar 3 A natural and the key of F major are restored. A
natural has the first success in the struggle by capturing the
second subject whose key is A major, the more normal key of C
being reserved for the second movement. In the third movement a first subject in C minor is followed by a second subject
in the key of A flat. A flat is now predominant and the finale
opens in the thundery key of F minor with a prominent A flat
in it. For conclusion however the symphony struggles back
to F major—A flat has been ejected after a prolonged combat,
which seems to suggest that ' frei aber froh ' is not such a simple
matter after all and the phrase means more than it says.

In the fourth symphony after a first movement with its
suggestion of variations interpenetrating sonata form, a simple
slow movement is followed by an ordinary scherzo—the only
one in Brahms (unless one includes his appassionato movement
in the second piano concerto in that category), rumbustious
and frivolous with piccolo and triangle.[1] Then comes the great
passacaglia on a theme derived from one of Bach's Church
Cantatas. At the thirteenth variation the key changes from
E minor to E major ; at the sixteenth the theme is given out
again in its original form as the introduction to a further fifteen
variations, capped by a coda in which Brahms allows himself
a greater measure of freedom, though he nevers goes very far
from his theme or from his established method of treating it.

Between Beethoven and Brahms came Schubert and a development of the programme symphony for which Beethoven had
established a precedent in the ' Pastoral '. Under this heading
may be placed Schumann's Rhenish, Mendelssohn's Scottish
and Italian, and Berlioz's Fantastic Symphonies.

Schubert wrote eight symphonies and sketched one other
which has since been completed by J. F. Barnett in the last,

[1] See Appendix II.

and by Weingartner in the present, century. His juvenilia are
not often heard, but No. 4, named the 'Tragic', and No. 5 are
sometimes played as an alternative to repetitions of No. 7 and 8,
the " Great C major " and the " Unfinished " respectively.

Schubert's is a more melodious way of writing symphonies
than Mozart's or Beethoven's as far as first movements are
concerned, though the first subject of the C major symphony is
mainly rhythmic in significance. But it is his transitions between the two subjects that show the different conception he
had of the use to which the form could be put. There is no
gradual leading from one key centre to another, as in Beethoven,
over a long bridge passage ; on the contrary his favourite plan
is to stand still for a few bars, pivot on his heels, face in the new
direction, and off and away on a new tune. The themes of the
' Unfinished ' are formal tunes, those of the C major are mostly
duets in thirds. But in spite of this sectional treatment—their
architectural plan is clear at a glance—their structure is firm
enough, although cuts are sometimes surreptitiously made in
the ' heavenly lengths ' of the C major. The lyrical ' Unfinished ' has won a place for itself in every heart, but the
C major is more truly symphonic—the fact that the ' Unfinished ' stops short at two movements indicates that its design
and its argument do not lend themselves to full symphonic
development. Furthermore the C major has a greater driving
power in the store of rhythmic energy which it seems to draw
from its opening (and it must be confessed somewhat bald)
tune on the horns, which develops a wonderful propulsive
speed by the time the finale, with its four reiterated minims,
has been reached. The opening phrase on cellos and basses in
the ' Unfinished ' might seem to be even more pregnant and to
contain greater possibilities, but it is not so. Perhaps a clue
to the deficiency (if one can speak of defect in anything which
is in itself so satisfying) may be found in the practical difficulty
in performance of striking speeds sufficiently differentiated for
a first movement marked *allegro moderato* and a slow movement marked *andante con moto*. They tend to approximate.
Weingartner makes little difference in the two tempi and
Furtwängler appears to have slowed down his first movement after a quicker start so that when he begins the andante
still more slowly the general effect is a running down of
energy through the symphony. Boult makes the andante a

little slower, and so does Beecham, which is correct, but the danger then looms up of losing the steady flow implied in the composer's mark *con moto*.

THE PROGRAMME SYMPHONY

The programme symphony differs from a 'straight' symphony as Beethoven's Sixth differs from his Fifth. There is a programme in both—it would be difficult even for a purist to deny some sort of psychological drama to the C minor symphony—but in the Sixth the programme is avowed. On the other hand the classical forms are preserved and the logic of real life—cause, sequence, chance, impulse—gives way to the preservation of symphonic logic—key relationship, phrase length, development and so on. In the symphonic poem the case is reversed and musical form goes as far as it can to meet the claims of the logic of the events described. There is no hard and fast line, and composers sometimes think of the music first and attach the programme afterwards, as Schumann admits to doing in the case of his first ' Spring ' symphony, and as we may suspect Tchaikovsky did to the elaborate explanation of the content of his fourth symphony. In his ' Rhenish ' symphony Schumann seems to have started with the impressions gathered from a visit to Cologne and in its fourth movement to have consciously aimed at descriptive reporting— we are shown a grand ceremony in the cathedral. Mendelssohn, who also wrote geographical music, completely absorbed his impressions before translating them into blameless symphonic form. Berlioz, who was even more a grand romantic personality than merely a romantic composer, was more self-conscious in his aims, but since he sometimes borrowed previously written music to fit into his schemes, his elaborately detailed programme of his Fantastic Symphony must not be taken literally as the inspiration and the determining factor in the composition of the music. The March to the Scaffold (the fourth movement) came from the opera, *Les Francs Juges*. It would be wrong however to regard the putting together of the movements of the symphony and the invention of a programme for them as so much deliberate fraud or even as rough carpentry. A whole congeries of thought, images, and emotions seethes together in the imagination and ultimately a flash of intuition fuses them. The root of this symphony describing

" An episode in the Life of an Artist " is no doubt autobiographical ; it opens with a tune associated with his boyhood's love for Estelle, and there is some reason for thinking that the *idée fixe*, which is announced at the beginning of the allegro immediately after the slow autobiographical introduction, is similarly rooted in his own experience.   What finally pulled the symphony together was an episode in his love for Harriet Smithson.   In February 1830 he wrote to a friend " I am about to commence my grand symphony in which the development of my infernal passion will be depicted ".   The basic musical idea was there, the extra-musical stimulus to create the symphony was provided, some of the music was already in existence; it only remained to get the actual plot clear.   Berlioz then elaborated his story of a young musician of abnormal sensibility who drugs himself with opium and with dreams of his beloved. The second movement is a valse and represents a ball where he once more finds his beloved.   In the pastoral third movement he is calmed by the sights and sounds of the country.   In the fourth he dreams he has murdered his beloved and is on the way to suffer for it on the scaffold.   The finale is a Witches' Sabbath in which lover, beloved, ghouls and monsters are all mixed up in a dance of death to the *Dies Iræ*.   A nice ultra-romantic subject for the august form of the symphony !   Some hold that it is the worst symphony ever written, but those who like their Berlioz like its peculiar tint and texture.

The fourth symphony of Tchaikovsky, though as far from it in tint and texture as Russia is from France, really runs on very much the same lines.   There is an *idée fixe* which appears in the first and last movements, the motif of Fate, and Tchaikovsky, has provided a detailed programme to explain its workings, though his ingenuity fails him for the scherzo (the pizzicato movement), and he confesses that in it no definite feelings are expressed.   The fifth symphony in E minor is really the same story over again with another fate-charged motto theme and a pervasive atmosphere of doom through four movements, such as enabled M. Massine to devise his ballet, *Les Présages*, to fit it without much violence to the music.   The ' Pathetic ' is perhaps even more personal.   Tchaikovsky was a neurotic and his hyperæsthesia blew off the emotional safety-valve at a comparatively low pressure.   Yet there can be no question of the validity of these personal explosions as works of art.   His choice and order of movements in the 'Pathetic' is worth noting. His first and third are the biggest but they show his weakness in development for which he falls back on reiteration. His scherzo is a gracious movement in 5/4 time, one of the earliest instances of a true 5/4 rhythm written out as such, and he reserves his slow movement for finale. This is indeed a movement of despair. Tchaikovsky's orchestration always gives a fully saturated sound, unlike the thinness of Berlioz, without its becoming turgid. Thus it is possible to give a translucent performance of the sixth symphony—Weingartner does it—and his use of the wind is individual and very happy. He seems to feel the wood-wind almost as though they were persons and not colours on a palette. His three earlier symphonies[1] are rarely played, but alongside of the symphonies have to be set a number of symphonic poems, which by the seventies of the century afford an alternative form to the composer of symphonies.

THE NATIONALISTS

Contemporary with Tchaikovsky and following a similar course of development was a composer from another branch of the Slav race, Dvorak the Bohemian. He too, like Tchaikovsky, used the symphonic form, evolved by German minds, for the expression of Slavonic ideas in Slavonic idiom, and on the whole successfully reconciled the Slav and Teuton elements in a new and distinctive product. Indeed he went further and by adding a further ingredient of negro folk idioms produced his best known and best-liked work, the Symphony from the New World. Only a composer of genius could have welded together such disparate elements in the crucible of his imagination to create a first-class work of art. Of his nine symphonies the first four were published posthumously but are not much played outside Bohemia. The numbering begins therefore at No. 5 which is usually called the first. The second in D minor and the fourth in G are to be met with in the concert hall, the latter especially showing in the happiest possible way the fertilizing influence of Czech folk-song and folk-dance, yet imposing no strain on the symphonic form and manner of treat-

---

[1] The 'Little Russian', No. 2, and the 'Polish', No. 3, have been recently recorded for gramophone under the stimulus of his centenary celebrations in 1940.

ment, as undigested folk tunes invariably do when they are borrowed directly for use as thematic material for symphonic development. The fact is that a folk-tune is a complete organism in itself; it is not therefore capable of further development. Thematic material on the other hand is chosen for its potentialities rather than for its immediate tunefulness. This incompatibility between two sorts of melodic material constituted one of the major problems of music during this period, when nationalism in many countries was challenging the supremacy hitherto exercised by Germany and Italy, and folk melody seemed the most obvious way of asserting national independence.

The Russians appear to come as near as anyone to solving the problem of the symphonic use of folk material, though Mr. Gerald Abraham points to Rimsky-Korsakov's Sinfonietta on Russian Themes as a demonstration of the impracticability of doing it. Tchaikovsky quotes the folk-song " In a field stood a birch-tree " in the fourth symphony as part of the second subject of the finale, whose opening also shows that ' barbaric ' touch of the Tartar which we Western Europeans always expect to find under the skin of the Russian. But Borodin, who does not quote a single folk-song, speaks the national and traditional language of Russian music in his B minor symphony much more clearly. One recognises the Russianness of Tchaikovsky as an individual but in Borodin one hears the voice of all Russia. His subject-matter is not personal but national. Here in the symphony are the same epic strains as in *Prince Igor*, the tunes have the same sort of national cut, and both the scherzo and the finale burst with the same sort of swishing energy as the Polovtsi Dances. Like Dvorak's, Borodin's tunes are impregnated with the essence of national folk-song and they coalesce into a symphonic texture all the better for not being genuine, self-subsistent folk-tunes. He had previously written a symphony in E flat and subsequently began one in A minor, of which only two movements were completed. Borodin was a great man, but his stature as a musician is not always recognised because he was an amateur and in the matters of orchestration he submitted to revision by Rimsky-Korsakov and Glazounov. His profession was that of a chemist, and he achieved such distinction therein that some of his processes are still in use. The intellectual grasp which he brought to his natural musical talent can be recognised in the symphony in the force and concision of the writing. Rimsky-Korsakov was more at home in the symphonic poem than in symphony proper, and his second symphony so-called is a work based on a programme, the Arab story of Antar furnished with quotations of real Arab folk-tunes, and is more truly described as a symphonic suite, like *Scheherazade.*

In fact the national school was less inclined to the symphony than the Moscow school, led by Tchaikovsky and the Rubinsteins, of which Rachmaninov is the surviving heir today. Glazounov, however, felt at home in the classical form and left no less than eight symphonies as well as concertos when he died in 1936. Dr. Colles devotes considerable attention to them in Vol. VIII of the *Oxford History*. Of the eight, the sixth stands the best chance of finding a place in our English repertory, the more so as Dr. Sargent has recently taken it up. The first movement for all its passion is neither strong nor dramatic ; it is in fact second-rate German music, written by a Russian. But it is offset by a delightful set of variations, differentiated from each other by a dominating orchestral colour and a specific type of musical form (fugato, scherzino, etc.) and by a truly Russian finale which is full of dazzling rhythmic contrivance.

Of the other nationalist schools with which Europe was filled in the second half of the nineteenth century neither Scandinavia, Hungary, nor Spain produced a symphonic literature. Neither Grieg, Bartok, nor Falla turned his mind towards the classic form of the symphony. Finland however produced Sibelius, of whom more later, and England stirring after the sleep of centuries, has brought forth a whole company of symphonists. The greatest of them, Edward Elgar, was no conscious nationalist ; he kept himself clear of the nationalist influences of the Tudor and folk-song revivals and shows more cosmopolitan traits than other Englishmen (except perhaps Bliss and Lambert), yet his are no German symphonies written by an Englishman in spite of his assimilation of Wagnerian harmony. They are however representative of their period, of the opulent Edwardian England when life was exuberant, expansive and confident. Elgar's A flat symphony, produced by Richter at Manchester in 1908, at once caught the ear of that generation and achieved the unprecedented feat of a hundred performances in its first year in spite of its length (50 minutes). It

begins with a quiet and confident motto-theme which pervades
every movement and is glorified in a grand re-statement at the
end of the finale, and it uses the same theme transformed à la
César Franck for scherzo and slow movement.   It has been
criticized on the ground of its discursiveness (which possibly
the composer felt able to indulge on the strength of the mechanical aids to unity just mentioned) and magniloquence.   The
magniloquence, symbolized in the frequent use of the expression mark *nobilmente*, is not to everyone's taste, its acceptability
depending in part on the quality of the performance.   The
second symphony in E flat, which came two years later, commands a wider and more unreserved acceptance now, though
at the time it did not make the same immediate appeal as its
predecessor.   It works from a brilliant opening to a serene
close, and it takes in on the way a Funeral March, which may
without improbability be connected with the death of King
Edward VII, to whose memory the symphony is dedicated.
There is more here of the wayward Elgar, greater clarity, and
some mellowing of the ardour as compared with the first symphony, but it is equally, perhaps more, representative of its
epoch in that it seems like an epilogue to it.

Parry and Stanford, the pioneers of the English revival both
wrote symphonies, but they have not remained in the repertory
and on a long view are less representative of their composers
than their vocal works.   For all their Englishness and Anglo-
Irishness they are not completely emancipated from German
thought-processes.   It was left for Holst (who wrote no symphony) and for Vaughan Williams (who has written three—
without counting the Sea Symphony which is really a cantata)
to secure national independence by rebuilding from the foundations of English counterpoint of the Elizabethan age and the
ageless melody of folk-song.   For Elgar in this respect ranks
as a post-Wagnerian.

Vaughan Williams flirts with, but runs away from, the idea
of a programme symphony in his London (1914) and Pastoral
(1921) Symphonies.   In the former he quotes the Westminster
chimes, and makes other allusions to London's sounds, such
as the hint of a mouth-organ in the scherzo (which is also a
nocturne—a bold combination of ideas since scherzos are always
quick and nocturnes usually dreamy).   But he says it ought
rather to be called ' Symphony by a Londoner ' than ' A London

Symphony' in order to leave himself a way of escape from the programme idea. Oh, these composers! Beethoven was equally misleading on the subject of his Pastoral Symphony. But in the case of Vaughan Williams the unstable equilibrium between the symphonic ideal and the topographical programme is to be explained by the composer's nationalist creed, which bade him look about him for inspiration and no longer go to Germany to study forms and methods. In the Pastoral Symphony there are no storms or cuckoos and only one really quick passage—the coda to the third movement, and that is pianissimo. Its mood is entirely contemplative—ruminative moments, such as occur even in the 'London', reflect the composer's most characteristic attitude—and it all seems to grow out of a four-note germinal motif. The countryside, which is the object of the composer's contemplation, would seem to be rather the bare but not forbidding Cotswolds where he was born than any of the softer English scenes, but he uses quite a luxurious orchestra for its depiction— three each of wood-wind and, as if that was not enough, a soprano voice in the finale. The F minor symphony (1931–4) provides the most complete contrast, for while it has no programmatic basis and is ostensibly devoted to a logical disquisition on two four-note subjects, it has a most pronounced emotional quality. It speaks of violence—the growing violence of the inter-war period. But it sticks closely to its text, the two motifs, of which one is as near a horizontal line as anything in music can be and the other as nearly vertical as a sequence of notes can be. The conclusion of the matter is a fugal epilogue on the horizontal motif. The symphony took the world by surprise by reason of its sheer brusque power, and those who regularly turn to the composer to voice their own quiet happiness in the strength and serenity and continuity of all things English were taken aback by this unexpected explosion. But that it reflected the spirit of the times in which it was written no one can deny. It was a symphony which spoke the blunt truth about the world we live in.

Bax has seven symphonies to his credit. In general they seem too diffuse quite to earn the high name of symphony, though they are most of them cast in some one or other of the modern developments of sonata form. His most interesting and personal modification of the form is his use of an epilogue (in Nos. 2, 3, 4, 5, and 6) on which he relies to unify the abundance of material he is inclined to load into his movements. If this good logical nexus is not always successful in conveying to the listener the sense of unity and coherence which he seeks, the reason is that Bax is fertile rather than selective in ideas and has an ear for full, saturated sound that leads to great richness of texture and of colour. Furthermore he does not know when to stop : he is constantly tempted to add another word to clinch the matter which in point of fact weakens rather than reinforces his argument. But if the symphonies are not sufficiently symphonic, if their logic is concealed by abundance of episode, they are at any rate rhapsodic, abound with lovely moments and glow continuously with orchestral colour.

The first symphony is however no easy-going rhapsody but a grim work that came out of the first German war. In it Bax seems to be not only grappling with some of the great heartsearching problems which that convulsion made urgent for all thoughtful people, but almost to be trying to exorcise some demon by looking it full in the face—a very good way of dealing with demons after all. Having then stated his problem in Symphony No. 1, the second is concerned to argue it out and the third to reach some sort of conclusion. No. 4 turns away from these urgent spiritual strivings to the contemplation of nature. But the mood of introspection and self-questioning returns in No. 5. The sixth is after a fierce first movement more lyrical, and the seventh, dedicated to the American people and first performed at the New York World's Fair in 1939, is again more extraverted and suggests some heroic saga.

Of other contemporary English symphonies those by Bliss, E. J. Moeran, and George Dyson are distinguished rather than compelling, but Walton's is nothing if not forceful. Its boldness in harmony, its rhythmic drive and its freedom in expanding, contracting and varying the material are held firmly together by the most primitive of all means, the pedal point. The seventh is a characteristic interval which is also used to give unity to the continually developing themes, for, oddly enough, the logical core of this modern symphony is the despised and rejected chord of the diminished seventh. Walton had some difficulty in finding an appropriate conclusion to his first three movements after the tense and bitter slow movement. The fugal finale came a year later and serves its purpose well enough, but it reverses the tendency of the previous century more and more to concentrate the weightiest matter of the symphony into the finale and returns to the classical practice of having the most substantial discussion first.

This notable and original work could hardly have been written as it stands if Sibelius had not been the predominant influence of the time when it was composed. Sibelius had been introduced to this country by Sir Henry Wood in the early years of this century before his music acquired the vogue that it now enjoys. His seventh symphony, written as long ago as 1925, has even now not been followed by a long promised eighth, and if Sibelius does not add anything to his varied output—for he has two distinct manners, a lighter dramatic and descriptive style and a more austere symphonic style, his seven symphonies between them cover a wide range of thought, and form in fact the richest and most concentrated achievement in the symphonic literature of to-day.

His general method is to work with short motifs which he assembles like pieces of mosaic; as he handles them they become integrated into the kind of complete themes from which normal classical procedure would have started. The first symphony runs fairly on orthodox lines, but in the most popular, No. 2 in D, the composer starts his reversal of classical procedure; in the exposition of the first movement the themes are bluntly stated, in the development they are built up into a whole and in the recapitulation dissolved once more into their elements. In the second movement another involution of classical procedure is adopted: the theme is stated, then hammered to pieces, and in the conclusion only its hard core handed back to the listener; the finale is more orthodox. Formally the most unusual of the series are No. 4 in A minor and No. 7 in C, which consists of one enormous movement. No. 4 indeed is the strangest symphony of modern times. It might have been composed on a telegraph form and scored as it stood. Yet its detached sentences hang together and the listener hangs upon their every word. Such concentrated logic leaves him dazed but not mystified. The third symphony on the other hand goes the other way to work; not in the least elliptical it makes its point by constant reiteration of its significant figures and it breathes a certain warmth of feeling. No. 5 in E flat is also an accessible work that makes a direct appeal. It is full of characteristic Sibelian features, tremolando scales on the strings, persistent reiteration of short melodic figures, many of them in thirds, like the horn tune in the finale. These reiterations stop abruptly when they appear to be well set and the symphony gives an impression of concision because it runs its first two movements together. No. 6 in D minor is the most elusive of the set. It is not so austere as No. 4 and includes in its score a harp and a bass clarinet, which is luxury indeed for a man of Sibelius's modest tastes, but it is cast in the Dorian mode, or rather in an ambiguous tonality based on D minor. It shows his increasing tendency to concentration and compression by stopping its four movements when the material has been sufficiently developed and it dispenses with formal recapitulation. Compression is carried still further in No. 7 in which the constituent sections of its single movement represent condensations of whole movements— slow introduction, allegro, scherzo and broad finale. The same thematic ideas run throughout, and not being abruptly dismissed give further cohesion to this further experiment in symphonic form.

All the processes of Sibelius's thought, choice of theme, formal presentation and instrumentation, sound startlingly different from any other music we know, yet their difference is not anything palpable. He indulges in no strange scales nor unconventional harmony, his form is unusual, as we have just seen, but it is all quite direct, and his orchestration, which sounds utterly remote from the orchestra of Strauss, his contemporary, contains no fancy instruments. His string writing often sounds eerie, yet the tremolando and pizzicato which are his chief licences are neither new nor extraordinary. The whole temper and colour, and indeed the substance of his music, is the product of his environment. It is not national but regional music— hyperborean. It is the expression of Finland because it comes from the depths of a Finn's mind, and it has all passed through the crucible before it is put on paper. Dr. Vaughan Williams said of it that Sibelius " makes the chord of C major sound more new and strange, more intensely individual than all the wildest polytonalities of the maddest mid-Europeans ". Sibelius almost admits as much himself when he says that instead of the multifarious cocktails offered by other composers he gives the public pure cold water.

We have arrived at the present day and find that modern

symphonies are to be found in Finland and in England. They
are also to be found in Russia, where Shostakovitch is the chief
name among the post-revolutionary generation. Prokofiev,[1]
a talented and prolific composer, tore up his roots and lived for
a time in Paris or U.S.A. If his music tended to become
desiccated and cosmopolitan, it yet retained his Russian humour
and naive melodiousness, as appears in his pretty parody,
the Symphonie Classique, and more recently in the neo-Aesopian
fable *Peter and the Wolf*. Shostakovitch derives more directly
from Tchaikovsky, but in his efforts to conform to Soviet requirements he appears to have lost his bearings. He has seven
symphonies to his credit of which only the first, which is the
most genuinely representative, is at all familiar to the British
public.[1] In France the most recent symphonist is Roussel who
left four symphonies of distinction, products of a fastidious
mind and not likely to become popular but rewarding to close
attention, such as may be paid to them through the gramophone.
Much the same can be said of Vincent d'Indy's three programme symphonies.

In pursuing the various offshoots of the main classical tradition which have led us to the outskirts of Europe I have omitted
to gather up the threads of German-Austrian symphony.
Bruckner and Mahler, who are regarded as heirs of the Viennese
school, have never had their numerous symphonies admitted
to the canon by Western Europe except at Amsterdam, where
Mengelberg has been a powerful advocate. Bruckner may be
described as a Wagnerian operating in the sphere of symphony,
though his own musical origin was the organ. His works
underwent considerable revision at the hands of friends and
conductors, and the publication of his own authentic versions
has led to a critical problem of some difficulty. English audiences
however are not likely to bother with it because even with
the cuts, which are among the subjects discussed, the symphonies
are over-long and over-ripe to their ears. Their lush romantic
character makes a special local appeal to Austrians, and, as has
been suggested by Dr. Colles, to virtuoso conductors who like
to " make something of them ".

Mahler, his contemporary and fellow symphonist—both
wrote nine—was such a virtuoso conductor and a many-sided
man into the bargain. He used words either for soloists or for

chorus or for both together in four of them, and he poured into the bursting form of the symphony every conceivable, and often inappropriate, idea that occurred to his lively fertile mind, including a good deal of quasi-philosophical bombast of the Teutonic kind, which was however the expression of deep religious self-wrestling and conviction. Where he excelled was in the simple and child-like ; of the symphonies, the fourth, which concludes with a child's vision of heaven described by a soprano soloist, is the most attractive to the normal English mind.

No successor to Brahms has appeared in North Germany. Strauss has devoted his energies to the symphonic poem and among the younger men of standing Hindemith has written no self-subsistent symphony, though he has collected some instrumental portions of his opera *Mathis the Painter* and issued them as a symphony with that title. The symphonic tradition, then, has branched out of its original stem, has shown great adaptability to national and temporal needs, and is still in as great a state of living flux as ever it was.

CHAPTER VII

CONCERTOS

AFTER the fairly comprehensive survey of the origin and development of the symphony in the last chapter it will be neither necessary nor desirable to examine the modern repertory of concertos so closely. It will be enough to take the chief types and observe how the general principles of instrumental music are applied to a form in which the idea of collaboration (symphony—voices in association) is modified to include in it that of a friendly contest (*certare*—Latin for to contest). A concerto is in fact a battle of unequal forces. The syllable *con* implies the ultimate reconciliation which is one of the æsthetic necessities of any instrumental music—nothing in music is simply eliminated ; it always has to be accounted for in the final reckoning.

The symphony, then, implies the co-operation and harmony of instruments, the concerto their friendly rivalry and contrast. For practical purposes concertos may be divided into two types : the concerto grosso of the eighteenth century and the solo concerto which grew out of it. The word is Italian and originally had a less restricted meaning than that which it bears as an English word today. Three centuries ago its English form was ' consort,' a term applied to the co-operation of instruments in chamber music. There is a good deal to be said for the revival of this word in its old sense as a substitute for the French ' ensemble ' which refuses to be acclimatized into our language. Concerto is comfortably at home as the designation of a work in which the virtuosity of one or more soloists is both pitted against and accompanied by an orchestra.

The element of virtuosity is essential. Even in the eighteenth century when the little orchestras at princely or ducal courts carried a number of passengers, servants or officials maybe, impressed to help out the second violins, the division into *concertino* and *ripieno* was at bottom a separation of the good players from those of more modest attainments. And so we find in the concerti grossi of Corelli, Handel, Bach, that the concertino players were given florid passages to play as a contrast to the straight-forward go-ahead ritornello (*i.e.* the principal, recurrent theme) in which the main body of players joined. The solo concerto encouraged virtuosity even more. Here is one individual who has to keep his end up against an impressive mass of orchestral sound. How is he to do it ? Only by brilliance and cleverness. All art is essentially doing or making, and what at the primitive level we all admire is just precisely the ability to do or make. Admiration for sheer skill is therefore a perfectly legitimate element in æsthetic appreciation. The word virtuosity gets into bad odour sometimes, because brilliance may be found associated with superficiality, with vulgar ostentation, with personal vanity and disregard for artistic values. In itself it is none of these things ; it is the possession of a certain kind of virtue. Anyone who can do anything supremely well, even if it is only balancing billiard balls on his nose, has virtue of some sort—patience and self-control among moral virtues for instance, muscular and nervous control among the physical virtues, and a willingness to amuse his fellow-men among the social virtues. Virtuosity makes an immediate appeal to us all and is an essential ingredient in all great art.

The concerto is the place set apart in music for the exploitation of this element. Concertos composed by great virtuosi however often fail to satisfy intelligent listeners because they are exploitations of technical virtuosity and nothing more. There is a whole library of concertos for the violin composed by famous players which make insipid hearing because they have nothing to them but a little facile melody and a lot of technical fire-works. The great composers Handel, Bach, Mozart, and in their younger days Beethoven and Brahms, were all first-rate executants, and in the eighteenth century the distinction between composer and performer, creator and interpreter as we now grandly style them, was not made. By the time of Brahms specialization had so far set in that composing music was found to be a whole-time job and the standard of public performance had become so exacting that it too called for all a musician's energies. When the great composers of the eighteenth century wrote concertos they brought to the task the double qualification of being great composers and of having a first-hand practical knowledge of their instruments. But when nineteenth century violinists wrote display pieces for themselves they had only a general musicianship and their executive skill to pit against the bigger minds and the creative impulses of the true composers from Beethoven through Mendelssohn, Brahms, and Tchaikovsky on to Sibelius, who might know less about the violin than de Bériot, Vieuxtemps, and Wieniawski, but had a deeper well of music in them on which to draw. A composer who is not a violinist but wishes to write a violin concerto may often consult a performer on the layout of particular passages, as Brahms consulted Joachim and Elgar (who was a violinist of moderate attainments) consulted Dr. W. H. Reed. So decided has the division of function become between composer and executant that now in the nineteen forties we only attend as a matter of courtesy to the compositions of executants, whereas even in the eighteen-seventies a performer's concerto might hope to gain a foothold in the concert repertory. Rachmaninov is the only exception.

A gramophone record has recently been issued of Paderewski's A minor piano concerto. Paderewski was a great man; even in the film with the rather naive story in which he recently took a part his personal greatness broke through the triviality, and his share in the rehabilitation of Poland after the 1914 war showed him to be a man of an altogether exceptional character. Any product of his mind is therefore bound to have some interest. He enjoyed a fair reputation before the last war as a composer. Yet there would seem to be little chance of a public revival of this concerto by some other pianist. This exclusive preoccupation with masterpieces of the highest rank is not altogether healthy. There is certainly an element of snobbery in it on the part of the public; there is the old British attitude that only the best is good enough for us, and there may be some blame attachable to critics who in their constant sorting and selecting come to attach too little importance to the second-rate. If the public persevered with Paderewski they would discover a distinctive voice in the finale, when the dash and colour of Polish national character expressed through the medium of Poland's great musician, virtuoso and patriot, makes music worth hearing.

In this category, but rather more secure of immortality come the concertos of two other composer-executants who were obviously remarkable men, Paganini and Liszt. In each case a certain *diablerie* of temperament finds expression in virtuosity that savours of wizardry. When an executant of equal wizardry comes along, who can punish their wickedly difficult works, even the most sceptical listener, to whom they are thoroughly uncongenial, is fascinated.

So much for instrumental virtuosity. It did not dominate the musical landscape in the days of the concerto grosso. Singers then had all the limelight. But distinctions were drawn between the concertino of superior players and the general orchestral mass called the ripieno. The supreme development of this particular balance of forces can be seen in Bach's Brandenburg Concertos, in the florid trumpet parts of No. 2, for instance, and in the magnitude of the pianist's solo in No. 5.[1] Earlier examples constructed largely on the same principle of having a ritornello (*i.e.* a returning theme) alternating with comment or variations or embroidery on it from the concertino players (generally violinists in the seventeenth century) show that another principle is involved as well as virtuosity, namely the sheer contrast of masses of tone. As early as Gabrieli, who died in the first years of the 17th century, contrast of tone, whether of different instruments such as strings with brass, or of dynamics such as alternate loud and soft and echo effects that sufficed as the chief kind of musical expression till the Mannheim school of orchestral playing—such contrast had an important bearing on the structure of instrumental music. Further contrast was obtained in the concerto grosso by having several movements of different character, speed and rhythm. Again, Bach shows these principles at their full development in the first Brandenburg, which ends with a string of formal dances after the normal sequence of allegro movements with a slow movement sandwiched between them.

One other feature to survive into the modern solo concerto which occasionally, though not invariably, was found in the eighteenth century concerto grosso is the cadenza. Handel left places in his organ concertos for extemporization—he wrote them for his own performance in the first instance—and marked a pause and the words *organo ad libitum* over the rests

---

[1] The instrument for which Bach wrote was not of course the piano, which had not long been invented, but the harpsichord. To-day, however, the part is played on a piano in forty-nine performances out of fifty. See pp. 123 and 127.

in the orchestral accompaniment.   In Bach's fifth Brandenburg
there is an elaborate solo for the pianist in the first movement,
but as Bach was executing a commission for the Markgraf of
Brandenburg and not writing for his own performance he did
not leave the cadenza to be improvised but wrote it out.
Improvisation was still a living art in the eighteenth century
practiced by singers who inserted *fioriture* (*i.e.* flourishes)
into the parts the composer had written for them, as well as
by organists, like Bach who had a reputation for it.   It has
now decayed and even in classical concertos where a cadenza
of some sort is prescribed by the composer and required by
the exigencies of form (as equivalent to the soloist's development section) we now wish we might be spared its execution.

It was Corelli (1652-1713) who did most to establish the
orchestral way of writing for violins ; his concerti grossi
are laid out for a concertino of two violins and a violoncello
supported by a ripieno of two violins, viola and bass.   One of
the best and best-known is the Christmas Concerto which contains an exquisite pastoral movement written for performance
on Christmas Eve.   Handel besides the organ concertos—
among them the famous and very jolly " Cuckoo and Nightin-
gale "—left Twelve Grand Concertos for a concertino of two
violins and violoncello accompanied by string orchestra and a
number of oboe concertos, improperly so-called since flutes
and bassoons are also employed.   Bach's six Brandenburg
Concertos show the greatest variety of instrumentation of any
surviving concerti grossi.   Two of them, Nos. 3 and 6, are for
strings only and these show less of the idea of antithesis and
contrast than the others ; they consist in fact of fugal movements on a single theme.   No. 3 is laid out in ten parts, three each
of violins, violas, and violoncellos with a basso continuo.   No. 6
is in six parts for two violas, two viole da gamba, violoncello
and double bass with continuo.   They show by their very limitation of orchestral colour what Bach's ideas were of orchestration.   He had an acute sense of colour and we are told that
as an organist he delighted in what would nowadays be described
as ' fancy ' stops, but his method of using colour was to choose
carefully what was appropriate to his ideas of the moment and
thereafter work with those colours only ; they were threads of
varied hue woven right through the texture, unlike the modern
method which seeks an ever-changing iridescent sheen.   These

two string concertos, No. 6 especially, show what richness of hue as well as of texture may be obtained merely by grouping the various string instruments then available—for the viola da gamba was not at that time quite obsolete.

No. 1 shows a similar exploitation of wind instruments— two horns, three oboes and bassoon and a sharp-toned violin, the obsolete violino piccolo, which is tuned a minor third higher than an ordinary violin. In this concerto as in Nos. 4 and 5 there is more contrast of masses ; in No. 5 there is more call for solo virtuosity, in No. 4 a violin has most of the florid work to do, dancing as it were to the piping of two flutes with which its solos alternate and contrast and combine.

These Brandenburg Concertos stand at the parting of the ways ; they mark the point at which chamber music and orchestral music diverge ; they mark the culmination of the old unitary and binary forms before they were superseded by sonata form ; they mark the supreme point of development of the old style of orchestral scoring in which the string and wind choruses played the same themes and the same type of music, a method soon to be discarded in favour of differentiating the characters of the various instruments and writing for them accordingly. Their robust health, alike in their vigorous first movements, their more contemplative slow movements, and their bustling finales, makes them an unfailing refreshment of spirit to hear. But they should not be played one after the other, or more than two in any one programme.

The concerto grosso idea passed away in the mid-eighteenth century in favour of the solo concerto, of which Bach himself left a number for violin and clavier (generic name for keyboard instrument and including clavichord, harpsichord, and pianoforte.) Quite recently it has been taken up again by modern composers, though they do not style the works in which they embody the idea concerti grossi. Such a composition as Elgar's Introduction and Allegro for string quartet and string orchestra is based on the principle of finding an equilibrium between unequal masses. Bliss's Music for Strings similarly depends for its textural interest on the subdivision of the string orchestra into various blocks and on the antiphony between them so obtained.

THE SOLO CONCERTO

The solo concerto was taken in hand by Mozart who left over fifty compositions for various solo instruments with orchestral accompaniment: ten for the solo violin, twelve for wind instruments (three for flute, one for clarinet, one for oboe, one for bassoon, and six for horn), and twenty-five for piano. In addition he wrote a number of double concertos; one for two violins, one known as the Sinfonia Concertante for violin and viola, one for flute and harp, one for two pianos, and one for three pianos. What, historically speaking, Mozart achieved in this extensive corpus of solo concertos was to find a place in the newly established sonata form for a soloist, who must not only have his share in the exposition and development of the material, but must be given scope for the display of his virtuosity. This is a bigger problem than had confronted Bach who had, for the most part during his employment with the Prince of Anhalt-Cöthen, written solo concertos for violin (two), clavier (four), the double concerto for two violins, two concertos for two pianos, two for three pianos, and one for four pianos. He wrote in the unitary form, in which the solo material is derived from the ritornello. The ritornello may be contrapuntal in texture; it recurs whole or in part through the movement, moving through a circle of nearly related keys, breaking off to allow the soloist his say and ending as it began with soloist and orchestra agreed in stating the main theme in a resounding accord. This was also the way in which Bach wrote a big vocal aria, and other composers, such as Haydn, when they wrote concertos seem to have conceived them as elaborate arias.

Mozart's method broadly speaking was to open with an orchestral tutti in which most of the material (not necessarily all of it) of the movement is stated in the main key. After this exposition the soloist restates it in his terms, amplifying and making the appropriate changes of key for the second subject. This section of the movement corresponds to the second statement of the exposition which in a symphony the orchestra makes when it reaches the double bar and, observing the direction to repeat, goes back to the beginning. In the course of the development section a place will be found for a second solo. In the recapitulation orchestra and soloist combine to give a compressed re-statement of the material. Something like a second development however is undertaken by the soloist on his own account in the unaccompanied cadenza which occurs just before a short final tutti. Tutti and solo thus roughly alternate, the orchestra leading each time but shortening its statements at each of its interventions. What opens as an expansive statement finishes compactly after sufficient opportunity has been allowed to the solo instrument for his own discourse upon it.

The second and third movements are generally built to a smaller scale. Three is the normal number of movements; Brahms's inclusion of a scherzo in his second piano concerto was an innovation which has not been generally imitated. Sometimes a scherzo is substituted for one of the other movements, as by Walton in his viola concerto which is designed on an unusual plan with the slow movement first. The slow movement may be a set of variations or a song-like movement and in Mozart the finale is generally a lively rondo. In his big C minor concerto (K 491) however he reverses this order : for slow movement he has a gentle rondo whose main theme lends itself to simple decoration, and he finishes with a set of variations.

Beethoven found Mozart's general design congenial to his thought for all but his last two great piano concertos. Indeed his C minor piano concerto (Op. 37) has been regarded as a model of concerto form, Mozart's form with its i's dotted and t's crossed. Sir Donald Tovey has been so anxious that the blue-print attitude to concerto form shall be avoided that he declares (a) that Mozart did not really use the form as it has been described above, and (b) that Beethoven, having used it once in this C minor concerto discovered that it was a mistake and never used it again. But Tovey is not consistent, and in individual analyses (See *Essays in Musical Analysis* Vol. III) makes numerous exceptions and admissions which weaken the force of his too drastic repudiation of the conventional view. He is certainly not entitled to deduce from the fact that Beethoven did not repeat his C minor concerto that he was dissatisfied with it. Actually the violin concerto (Op. 61) which came after the G major piano concerto in which Beethoven broke away from the convention of the opening tutti, is written according to Tovey's own analysis on the Mozartian plan, though its scale is vaster and its style, maybe, more symphonic.

In the G major and E flat ('Emperor') piano concertos Beethoven assigned to the solo instrument instead of the orchestra the important task of opening works of the greatest magnitude. The effect is dramatic in the G major concerto and imparts a dramatic twist to the whole work which issues in the impassioned dialogue of the slow movement—a movement which has been likened to the colloquy of Orpheus with the frontier guards of the Underworld. In the ' Emperor ' the effect is rhapsodic and introduces a concerto drawn on an epic scale. Brahms in his second piano concerto begins with a duet between a horn and the piano, and in the double concerto for violin and violoncello allows his soloists an early opportunity of taking part in the exposition, but in his first piano concerto and in the violin concerto he begins with an orchestral tutti.

The practice however of bringing the soloist in at once or very early in the movement received support from Mendelssohn, who in his two piano concertos and in the violin concerto in E minor simply suppressed the opening tutti. The solo violin takes charge from the outset and proves fully capable of expounding a long and well organized first subject with no more than a helpful accompaniment from the orchestra. The soloist however allows the orchestra to have the first statement of the second subject in the key of the relative major, but in general the orchestral tutti is reduced in importance and serves mostly as a strong connecting link between the various sections of the movement. The general effect of this treatment is to reduce both the size and the weight of the first movement ; so much so that Mendelssohn was able to join all three movements of the violin concerto by orchestral transitions without overweighting a structure which thus falls into three approximately equal parts. A good many concertos of the romantic period similarly lightened their first movements by modifying the opening tutti with an immediate appearance of the soloist. Max Bruch's familiar violin concerto in G minor, for instance, labels its first movement a Prelude, and Schumann's piano concerto, though the first movement is drawn on a large scale, actually began life as a fantasia for piano and orchestra. By the time one gets to Tchaikovsky and Rachmaninov the first movement has become inflated, but the design, with the piano to the fore in the exposition, is not on the grand classical scale of, say, Brahms's violin concerto. The modern practice in general is to allow the soloist to make an early appearance, and to reduce the orchestra's part from symphonic to subservient status.

This shift in the balance of power may be due in part to the actual increase in the orchestral forces. The modern pianoforte is a loud-mouthed enough orator in all conscience but when he is pitted against the modern symphony orchestra with its trumpets, trombones and tuba, as he is in Tchaikovsky's B flat minor concerto, the handicapping must not give the orchestra a long start of ·him if he is to keep his end up. Honours are generally regarded as even for this concerto, which is affectionately known as the " bloody but unbowed," the epithets unquestionably referring, despite their grammatical connexion with the concerto, to the condition of the soloist at the end of it.

In the repertory of concertos those for piano far exceed in number those for any other instrument, and among concertos ought also to be included a number of works in other forms but containing big parts for piano solo in antithesis to the orchestra. Such works are the *Variations Symphoniques* and the symphonic poem *Les Djinns* of Franck, Falla's *Nights in the Gardens of Spain*, Rachmaninov's Paganini Rhapsody (actually a set of variations), and Strauss's Burlesca.

Before the general acceptance of the piano at the end of the eighteenth century the keyboard instrument in general use was the harpsichord. Bach's clavier concertos were intended to be played on the harpsichord and their accompaniment is light— for strings only. He left four concertos for one clavier, two for two claviers, two for three claviers and one for four, though this is a transcription of a work for four violins by Vivaldi and the others are not all original works for keyboard instruments. It is a little difficult for the layman to keep track of Bach's various concertos as he had a habit of rewriting them in different keys for different instruments. Thus both the violin concertos are found in two transposed versions for clavier, and even the great double concerto for violins in D minor is found in another key arranged for two claviers. In his Leipzig days he contributed to the concerts of the University Musical Society, and sometimes drew on his own earlier works, as well as on transcriptions which he made of Vivaldi's violin concertos. This may well account for the existence of many of his concertos in more than one form. Outstanding however are the concertos originally composed in D minor for one clavier, in C major for two, in D minor for two violins, and in C major for three claviers with its buoyant and triumphant finale. His transcription for four claviers of Vivaldi's concerto for four violins inevitably loses much in the process—notably in the slow movement where each violin maintains against its fellow a consistent type of figuration and bowing, a counterpoint, as it were, of violinistic figures. But Bach showed a curious insensibility to the finer shades of suitability—he constantly transferred music composed for one set of words to others quite different with complete disregard of the distinctions of sacred and secular. It was the substance of the music that mattered to him, and in the concertos it is the substance that we get, no matter what the instrument to which it was first assigned.

Haydn in the seclusion of Esterhaz wrote a number of concertos, including several for piano of which only three have been published. The most familiar is one in D which has a so-called Hungarian finale. Brahms was fond of these Hungarian finales and included a theme of Hungarian cut in the first episode of the final rondo of his B flat piano concerto. In Haydn's concerto the folk influence is not even Hungarian but Slavonic, but it makes a crisp and sprightly conclusion to a light-fingered little work.

Mozart's piano concertos fall into three groups ; the first four early works and adaptions at that, the next six composed during his residence in Salzburg between 1773 and 1777, and the last fifteen written at Vienna after 1782, works of his maturity and comparable in depth with the symphonies of the same period. Most of these piano concertos Mozart wrote for his own performance at the various subscription concerts he gave in Vienna from time to time to raise a little much-needed money. He had greater affection for the piano than for the violin, which he only played in his Salzburg days, and while the early violin concertos stand for purity, the piano concertos are distinguished for their riches—riches of feeling and riches of imagination to fill out the same design but on a larger scale. Even in a comparatively early and comparatively light work like the A major concerto of 1782 (K414) the first movement has a certain spaciousness and the slow movement is based on a deeply expressive melody of sustained feeling. But four years later when he wrote the C minor concerto he strikes a deeper and more dramatic note, as so often when he writes in the minor mode. From an almost tragic first movement he passes to a child-like slow movement, a simple rondo in the relative major, and then back to a set of variations, masculinely diatonic and passionately chromatic by turns, in the original emotional key of C minor.

Of the later concertos the best known are the three composed in the course of a single year, 1786, which are comparable to the three great symphonies which he was also to produce within a similar period in the year 1788. There are besides the C minor already discussed, one in A (K488) and one in C (K503). A later work, the Coronation Concerto in D (1788), was written more as a business speculation than from inner compulsion, and though a work of some size it is formal in manner and superficial in quality. The last in B flat belongs to 1791 : like most of the music written in these last years of his short life it has its shadows.

Of Beethoven's five piano concertos something has already been said about the last three, which overshadow the two earlier ones in C major and B flat. ' Emperor ' is a title given in England to the majestic concerto in E flat but the Viennese will not know what you mean if you speak of Beethoven's *Kaiser Konzert*. Its balance of keys is one of the most interesting things about it, since it begins with a great plunge to the subdominant, and extreme measures have to be taken before the end to restore an equilibrium which has been biassed early and powerfully towards the flat side of its tonic. No. 4 is the most poetical concerto ever written for the piano, not excluding Schumann's which abounds in feminine virtues. It is noteworthy that on the whole these two concertos are better played by women than men. The ' Emperor ' on the other hand, like Brahms's two colossal examples, is essentially masculine in character and responds best to a man's hand.

Chopin's two concertos in E minor and F minor come dangerously near to the insipidity of the virtuoso performer's composition. Chopin could hardly commit an infelicity for the piano, but he had considerable difficulty in filling out a symphonic form and his handling of the orchestra was not particularly expert. Schumann's is the romantic concerto par excellence and no one would guess that several years intervened between the composition of the first and the last two movements, it all seems so inevitable and the scoring, which in Schumann's symphonies tends to be thick and chunky, is so apt and so full of the most captivating touches—think, for example, of the way the clarinet picks up the first subject tune at the recapitulation in the first movement and recall the cross rhythm of the strings in the finale. Grieg's solitary essay in concerto form ought not perhaps to be mentioned in the same paragraph with it, yet besides sharing the key of A minor it opens in the same youthful way and keeps its freshness and ardour undiminished.

The romantic movement however threw up one other development. Liszt for his two concertos in E flat (the "Infernal Triangle") and A, contrived to compress the three normal movements into a single-movement concerto, in which the last part becomes a kind of recapitulation of the first through the device of a transformation of themes. The same theme appears in the different sections suitably disguised in rhythm and tempo to reflect the different moods, and in the last part to resume its adventures and developments in a glorified re-statement. This Lisztian plan was adopted by Saint-Saens more than once.

Nationalism has not been particularly prolific in piano concertos. Besides Scandinavia as represented by Grieg, there is only Russia as represented by Tchaikovsky, the now forgotten Rubinstein, Glazounov and the much played concertos of Rachmaninov. Of these there are four excluding the Paganini Rhapsody. No. 2 in C minor is the most familiar and is on the whole the best because, although its neurotic atmosphere repels some people, it is entirely sincere and represents the composer's victorious struggle from a breakdown with the help of the physician to whom it is dedicated. No. 1 in F sharp minor is the shortest and was re-written during the days of the revolution in Moscow; it suffers from too much obsession with the single mood of lyrical self-pity. No. 3 in D minor abounds in passages that show the composer's own pianistic virtuosity prompting and suggesting ideas to him : it is essentially pianist's music. Delius, the cosmopolitan, has a single uncharacteristic and not very good piano concerto among his earlier works. Ravel is France's modern representative with two concertos both belonging to the same year—1931 : one of them is a singular and rather attractive concerto for left hand alone ; the other in G for the less exacting virtuosity of two hands aims, in his own

words, not at profundity or dramatic effects but at lighthearted-
ness and brilliance. Too many concertos, he added, appeared
to be composed not so much ' for ' as ' against ' the piano.
His own texture is sufficiently attenuated to avoid that reproach.
Saint-Saens, who wrote five concertos for piano, is a classicist
who says what it is not worth saying perfectly. They have
elegance and a certain bright euphony. They are no doubt
excellent fun to play and can be made to sound effective if only
the pianist can contrive to conceal their hollowness. English
composers have been chary of the form. Vaughan Williams
alone, since the days of Mackenzie's rather jolly Scottish Concerto, has ventured on a concerto, in which he assigns a particular style, we might almost say a particular period, to each movement, the early toccata manner of the harpsichord in the first,
romantic arpeggios in the second, and the modern dynamic
style in the last movement.

A few moderns have written whole concertos in the style
that treats the piano as an instrument of percussion—Constant
Lambert for instance with a small chamber orchestra and Prokofiev on a bigger scale in no less than five concertos to date,
but all this stuff is drier than dog-biscuit, though Prokofiev
serves it up with a sauce of wit. The percussive way of regarding the piano that contemporary fashion has borrowed from
jazz has legitimate possibilities no doubt, and the resources
of pianism have been enlarged by their adoption, but the piano
is essentially an illusionist, a singer that cannot really sustain
his tones but has always succeeded in the illusion that he can—
for art thrives on its own limitations—and we shall not get
much satisfaction from the modern piano concerto until composers do as Vaughan Williams has done and recall its other
than purely percussive abilities.

The repertory of concertos for the violinist is much more
restricted than that for the pianist. He has two supreme
masterpieces—the concertos of Beethoven and Brahms, to
which those of Mendelssohn and Elgar may be added. Bach
left two solo concertos of small calibre. Mozart's violin concertos are all early works written when the composer was still
employed at Salzburg. He never lavished on them the same
warmth of feeling as he did on the piano concertos and never
seems to have cared greatly for the violin ; he gave it up in later
life in favour of the viola which he used to play in chamber

music. But the concertos have a limpid purity and are pleasing in the ' galant ' style. Excluding single movements, and two concertos of doubtful authenticity—that in E flat (K268) and the so-called ' Adelaide ' concerto—there remain five early works and one recently recalled from obscurity by the Roumanian violinist and composer, Enesco, and his pupil, the prodigy Yehudi Menuhin. This is numbered No. 7 in D and was only published in 1907—130 years after it was written ; in spite of the appeal of its slow movement and the headlong impetus of the finale it never caught the fancy of players or public. Another recent resurrection has been Schumann's violin concerto disinterred in 1937 against the express and well-founded decision of the composer and his best friend to bury it. Bruch's is a capital work of the second rank, superficial but pleasing, the sort of work that has its own national appeal but would hardly have gained its place of favour in this country but for the German domination of English taste during the nineteenth century. Tchaikovsky and Sibelius represent the nationalists. Respighi has brought back Italy once more after two centuries into the European concert of string music with his Gregorian Concerto. Saint-Saens the encyclopædic, the modern Mozart without Mozart's virtue, has of course written concertos for violin as for piano and violoncello, and of the three the third in B minor is most often heard. The greatest of modern concertos is undoubtedly Elgar's—a work of complex structure drawn on a large scale but full of poetry, based on themes of individual melodic cut that could only have come from one mind and striking the classical balance between soloist and orchestra that is elsewhere found only in Beethoven and Brahms, a balance symbolized in the fact that the soloist has only one cadenza, which does not occur till the finale and which when it occurs is accompanied. This was written in 1909. Since then two more English works have been composed for violinists ; Vaughan Williams's Concerto Academico with accompaniment for string orchestra, described as "Bach gone wrong " and owing its title to its style, which certainly throws a backward glance at the eighteenth century while speaking the idioms of the twentieth; and the concerto of large design which Walton wrote for Heifetz and which was heard at the New York World's Fair in 1939, but was not "generally released " or played in England till late in 1941.

Prokofiev has written two concertos for violin which show the wit and quick resource of his mind. Though the melodic quality of the solo instrument is some safeguard against the recurrent aridity of the piano concertos, he does not wholly succeed in sustaining what often promises to be an interesting argument. Thus in the second concerto in G minor good melodic ideas peter out during their development into virtuoso arabesques, while the attempt to write in the finale rough percussive stuff, though modish and modern enough, is not really grateful to the instrument nor gratifying to the ear. It has even been called drab, though that perhaps is a little harsh for the crackling ingenuities of so sprightly a composer.

Smaller still is the violoncellist's repertory though it contains one or two works that inspire peculiar affection. At the head of the list, and as lovable as Beethoven's G major and Schumann's piano concertos, is Haydn's in D, which is not by Haydn at all but by a pupil, Anton Kraft. It does not sound like Haydn —Tovey was always disturbed by the opening bars of the slow movement which he describes as a Mozartian cliché—" two bars of pure Mozart, followed by two of pure Haydn "—and the gently rolling tune of the finale has more a Bohemian than an Austrian cut, with its short phrases of two bars and one bar building up into an extended melody that sounds particularly gracious in the hands of women players. Mozart, who wrote something for almost every instrument, bequeathed no concerto to the violoncellist. Dvorak's concerto in B minor, though a longer work, has the same kind of Bohemian amiability as Kraft's. Schumann's is not so easy to get on with. Sheer shortage gives additional value to Saint-Saens's two essays in this form. Tchaikovsky's Variations on a Rococo Theme are graceful and decorative, making a work of less magnitude than a concerto, yet bigger than anything could be which had only a piano for partner ; it has all the prettiness implied in the adjective ' rococo ' and is music that sets out to please. Deeper emotions are stirred by Elgar's violoncello concerto—the last big work Elgar was to write. It came in 1919 just before Lady Elgar died, and though it is not a big work as size is counted and its orchestration is less brilliant than the composer uses elsewhere, it is a pearl of great price.

The viola has hitherto had nothing of its own, though it is an equal partner with the violin in Mozart's Sinfonia Concertante, and in Strauss's *Don Quixote*—which is the equivalent of a violoncello concerto in the realm of the symphonic poem—the viola joins with a tenor tuba in presenting the character of Sancho Panza. But one of the most noteworthy concertos of modern times has been written for an instrument neglected by everyone till Mr. Lionel Tertis raised its status by his masterly performance on it. Walton's viola concerto is cast in an unusual form in that it begins with a slow movement, followed by a scherzo—tart, dashing and incisive in Walton's most familiar style and finishes with a movement in which the threads are gathered together and the issues of the complex opening resolved in a contemplative and unexpectedly lyrical strain. Another English composer has given the violist a concerto in modern idiom—Elisabeth Maconchy, whose concerto was first played by Bernard Shore in 1938.

Wind instruments have such decided characters that the danger of monotony, especially monotony of tone colour and the limited figuration of which they are capable, has made composers chary of writing extended virtuoso works for them except under the influence of a special player. Mozart for instance was encouraged to write his clarinet concerto by the art of Stadler, though he had already been generous in the matter of wind concertos, having written no less than six for horn, three for flute, and one each for oboe and bassoon. The bassoon concerto (K 191) is a sparkling early work of his youth; its light-hearted and amusing strains may be set over against the almost morbid beauty of the clarinet concerto of his death year. The flute concertos come between (1778) and are light weights.

The flute has Bach's B minor Suite with string accompaniment and important roles in two of the Brandenburg Concertos, but has been cold-shouldered by the romantic composers. The oboe has done rather better in modern times, and under the stimulus of Mr. Leon Goossens's playing has received three recent concertos for its repertory from English composers, as already recorded (Chapter IV. p.41). The clarinet has two concertos as well as a concertino from the pen of Weber and another from Stanford. The bassoon has also a contribution from Weber and in recent years from Eric Fogg. The heavier wind does not go in for concertos, except the trumpet for which a few short pieces are available, including a concerto by Haydn.

There remains a class of works which seek to double or treble their attractiveness by offering duets or trios in place of solos. This is to go back in effect to the idea of the old concerto grosso in which a small group is set over against a large. But the form and the treatment of the most important works in this class after the time of Bach are those of the solo concerto. The two (or three) soloists discourse together, sometimes in antiphony, sometimes in harmony, but their relation to the orchestra, their common exposition of the material, follows the principles that govern the form of the solo concerto. The Sinfonia Concertante of Mozart is Mozart's own concerto form enlarged only in so far as the two instruments can together fill a larger framework without strain. Brahms's double concerto is for violin and violoncello ; it would hardly claim to be an easy or an accommodating work in which virtuoso display was a prime consideration. It wears in some performances even a forbiddingly austere aspect, but its challenge, its passion, and its sheer musical interest win and hold the listener, and there is a feeling of drama in the unequal struggle between a partnership of strings and the majestic orchestra.

Bach's concertos for more than one keyboard have already been mentioned. Emanuel Bach and Mozart also left concertos for two pianos, but the nineteenth century, the heyday of the solo piano, preferred not to spoil a good thing by doubling it. The recent interest in piano duets, stimulated again by eminent performers, Ethel Bartlett and Rae Robertson, may be expected to produce some extended work for this medium. So far Arthur Bliss's rewritten concerto for two pianos and a brand new Introduction and Allegro by Lennox Berkeley are the chief signs of awakened interest in this country. Neither France nor Germany, nor Cosmopolis, as represented for instance by Stravinsky, have so far been drawn to explore its modern possibilities, though Stravinsky scores his ballet, *Les Noces*, for four pianos and percussion. But ballet and concertos are distinct, not to say, distant fields of operations.

The triple concerto is, after the time of Bach, a rare bird. Beethoven perpetrated one for piano, violin and violoncello, which is less interesting as music than as an experiment in designing a concerto on a sufficiently large scale to accommodate so many important virtuosi. Modern experiments in multiple solos revert more to the concerto grosso type, and are generally drawn on smaller lines almost to the extent sometimes of emerging as glorified chamber music, which again is a withdrawal from the ideal of symphonized virtuosity.

CHAPTER VIII

DANCE, THEATRE, AND PROGRAMME MUSIC

THIS small book is not an encyclopædia. It contains a bird's eye view of symphonic literature, but it cannot attempt to pass in review the non-symphonic part of the vast repertory of the concert orchestra even with the superficial glance of a bird of passage. There is too much music in the world and there is a conspiracy among conductors to defeat the merciful provision of Nature whereby the unfit does not survive. New music comes clamouring for a hearing, but it has to compete not only against an excessive devotion to the great standard masterpieces but against revivals and trial runs of long neglected works. Every one of these tendencies is in itself healthy enough. The masterpieces deserve to be heard because they yield the maximum of spiritual satisfaction. New music deserves to be heard or the art will perish of sclerosis ; every generation has a right to express and record its view of the world in music as in art, politics or philosophy. Neglected music deserves to be heard, because it is right to take down from the shelf works relegated to it by our parents and grand-parents, especially as in matters of taste one age's meat is another period's poison. It is worth doing even if we, as an appeal tribunal, decide that the shelf is after all the right place for these candidates for renewed currency. But the accumulations of a mere four centuries are enormous and submerge the most resolute curiosity to master the literature of the orchestra, not to speak of the vast corpus of vocal and chamber and domestic music. One alleviation has lately appeared—the consumption of music has risen with the apparently insatiable appetite of the broadcasting microphone. There is a demand for a very great quantity of music. But it is more than any one man's work to have even a nodding acquaintance with all the wealth of orchestral music, light or serious, formal or romantic, self-subsistent or illustrative. Here we can do no more than glance at the various categories.

If there is any art prior to music, it is dancing. Perhaps music and dance are twin sisters, children of rhythm. At any

rate each has served the other.   Dance has called for music to
be piped unto her; music has borrowed the rhythms and forms
of the dance to make for herself tunes to sing and play.   One
great class of music has come to the orchestra from the dance—
the Chaconnes of Purcell, the Suites of Bach, the Divertimenti
of Mozart, the Waltzes of the Strausses, and now the infiltra-
tion of rag-time.

Music's other sister is the drama, and here again there has
been a mutual exchange of services.   Music constantly under-
takes quite menial offices to serve the theatre, but has requited
herself by swallowing the drama whole to make herself an
Opera.   The obvious contributions of the theatre to the orchestral repertory consist of the incidental music to plays.   Purcell
squandered his genius on Restoration drama, Beethoven ennobled
Goethe's *Egmont*, Mendelssohn stole from Shakespeare a whole
fairy-land to make a midsummer night's dream.   North European composers like Grieg and Sibelius have found inspiration
in the Scandinavian enthusiasm for the drama and have made
up suites like *Peer Gynt* and *The Tempest* from music written to
order for special productions.   Sometimes such music does not
survive to a longer and independent life ; thus Delius wrote
some music for Flecker's *Hassan* but no one has ever heard it for
it was not audible in the babel of the theatre and hardly robust
enough for a separate life.   Music in this class is always liable
either to immediate extinction or to sudden and perhaps permanent glory.

Dance and the theatre unite in the Ballet and ballet has in
the past century conferred some of the most exciting, highly
coloured and, of course, rhythmically stimulating, music upon
the   connoisseurs of the orchestra.   *Giselle* is the oldest
ballet in the repertory, having just reached its centenary, and
Adolphe Adam's music for it is charming, but too frail for
reproduction away from the stage.   Now and again, however,
conductors specializing in a search for light music find in scores
like those of *Giselle* and its kindred some selections that serve
their turn.   But coming on a little to the great days of the
Imperial Russian Ballet a whole world of enchantment is discovered by Tchaikovsky—*Casse-Noisette*, *Lac des Cygnes*, and
The Sleeping Princess.   Stravinsky follows with the unques-
tioned masterpiece, *Petrouchka*, and two worthy companions in
L'Oiseau de Feu and the challenging and much challenged

Le Sacre du Printemps. Many a work—including symphonies nowadays—has been butchered to make a balletomane's holiday, but ballet has made amends with Ravel's *Daphnis et Chloe*, with Falla's *Tricorne*, with Vaughan Williams's *Job*, and Bliss's *Checkmate*; so the tribute comes from Russia, France, Spain and England.

The Opera too brings its quota. True, the operatic pot-pourri has disappeared from the highest musical circles, but concerts of excerpts from the Wagnerian music-drama are still with us, and raise a problem of musical ethics. Apart from this —which must be thrashed out along with two other æsthetic issues, the ethics of transcription and the nature of programme music—opera contributes with unquestionable propriety the Overture, though there are overtures without operas like Mendelssohn's *Hebrides* and *Ruy Blas* and a whole bouquet of concert overtures.

Overtures from the theatre are of two sorts—those that refer thematically to what is to follow and those that do not. The earlier practice, which continued up to Mozart, was to make the overture independent, a development,—at how long a distance!—of beating the big drum before the show begins and of Monteverde's fanfares in C major before *Orfeo*. Mozart's *Figaro* is the consummate instance; here is no tragedy, but bustle, animation, intrigue and the sweetness that is not found in the play till the end. This type of overture is in a reduced sonata form, in which the themes are expounded and recapitulated fully and spaciously but not developed in a formal middle section. Weber established the practice of introducing salient themes from the subsequent opera in *Der Freischütz*, *Oberon*, and *Euryanthe* overtures, and was followed by Wagner in *Tannhäuser*, *Lohengrin* and *Meistersinger*. Beethoven went further and compressed the essence of the drama into the overture. In *Leonora No.* 3 he so far overdid this kind of introductory process as to make it unfit for its function as a prelude. But he succeeded unintentionally in writing the greatest of all concert overtures, and the trumpet call, whose function is as purely dramatic as a piece of stage business or a stage property, crowns the musical climax with a shock that never loses its power to startle and to thrill. The number of classical overtures which make the ideal *apéritif* to a concert is not enough to go round, and all the standard overtures by Mozart, Beethoven (which

belong more to drama than to opera) Weber, Wagner, Mendelssohn, Berlioz, Smetana and Dvorak are overworked. Vaughan
Williams's *Wasps* overture has been requisitioned; Elgar's
Cockaigne, though not quite so suitable for general purposes,
is splendid for special occasions. The need is greater than the
supply, since the artistic requirements of an overture are exacting. It must speak decisively and appealingly in small space,
it must have a certain dignity and importance however airy its
subject matter, since its function is to grip the attention of the
audience and attune its mind to bigger things to follow. It had
better be fleet of foot, and cannot afford to waste time or energy
in coming to its climax and finishing its business.

The largest single class of unsymphonic music for orchestra
consists of programme music, music, that is, written to illus-
trate directly some aspect of real life. If every picture tells a
story, it can equally be argued that every piece of music that
is not academic manipulation of material or the vapid product
of an empty mind, has some meaning, *i.e.* some meaning outside music, even if it is beyond the capacity of language to state
precisely what that meaning is. Mendelssohn argued convinc-
ingly that if what was to be expressed could be expressed in
words, it would not be put into music; and certainly no non-
musical interpretation of a piece of music is going to exhaust
the meaning of the music. But music must have a starting
point in the composer's experience of life, and it will in the
event tell us something about its creator's mind or temperament.
If it is to be of any interest, it must deal in the last resort with
the stuff of life itself. It is a first-class issue in æsthetics whether these statements represent the truth about absolute music,
i.e. symphonies, sonatas, variations, and other " purely musical "
forms. The contrary view is held by the best thinkers in
music who say that music is just music. This is not the place
to argue the issue[1] nor to explain that the essence of the creative
activity of the mind consists of intuition expressing itself in
symbols. Aristotle observed that it is the mark of the poetic
mind to note latent resemblances, to make comparisons, to coin
metaphors embodying these resemblances and comparisons,
to use one image, in fact, as the symbol of another, thus gather-
ing greater richness of meaning into an image of almost con-

[1] Readers who are interested will find the question argued in my *Key
to the Art of Music*. (Blackie).

crete substantiality, as when we talk of ' defending the flag ' or ' crowning a life-work '. Here the images of the flag and the crown have become symbols of a rich nexus of associated meanings. Musical imagery is only one kind of imagery—most people are visuals, some are motiles but musicians are audiles—but almost anything can be turned into the imagery of organized sound by a musical imagination, and crotchets and quavers become the symbols of almost anything— though propositions of Euclid, political dogma and scientific hypothesis cannot be expressed with precision in musical terms unaided by words. The addition of music to words, however, has always produced a very powerful form of statement, even of such recalcitrant material (from the musical point of view) as the theological dogmas of the *Credo* of the Mass, and Wagner embodied a whole social philosophy in his music drama of *The Ring*.

Whatever may be the nature of abstract music—whether it symbolizes something beyond itself or not—the nature of programme music is to express in musical terms all sorts of ideas, events, feelings, states of mind and even pictorial images. This sort of representation of the physical world has been a function of the most disembodied of the arts since composition began. The starting point, no doubt, is the imitation of the sounds of nature, from the song of birds to running water. For the representation of these natural phenomena music uses tone, melody and rhythm ; the bird-call can be imitated as to tone quality, its elusive rhapsody can be imprisoned in some more formalized though still far from formal melody, while the movement of water has a close analogue in the rhythmic movement of music. For music, like water, flows ; ' rhythm' is Greek for flow ; and any form of physical movement can be accurately pictured in the rhythm of sound. But programme music goes far beyond imitation. Even Byrd in the early days of keyboard instruments demanded of his virginals the representation of a battle, down to the details of marching and the burial of the dead. Bach's predecessor at Leipzig set the slaying of Goliath and the sickness of Hezekiah to music, Dittersdorf, the contemporary of Haydn, took the story of Phaethon from Ovid and converted it into a primitive symphonic poem ; Mozart wrote an orchestral piece about a thunderstorm before Beethoven put one into the Pastoral Symphony ; Strauss with a full modern orchestra imitates a flock of sheep in agitation in

Don Quixote, describes the arrest and execution of a rascal
(*Till Eulenspiegel*) gives an exposition of Nietzschean philosophy (*Also sprach Zarathustra*) and conveys the atmosphere of
death—you can smell ethyl chloride in the room—(*Tod und
Verklärung*).

If the idea of the symphonic poem is inherent in instrumental
music from the start, the actual title was Liszt's invention.
The similar idea of the programme symphony was adopted by
his contemporaries, Berlioz, Mendelssohn and Spohr. Liszt's
practice deviated from theirs in that he discarded the limitations
of symphonic form and allowed the poetical content of each
work to determine the form. ' Symphonic poem ' is therefore
a correct and adequate description of these large orchestral
works that are not symphonies. Liszt's own practice was to
take for subject a poem like Goethe's *Tasso* or a picture like
Kaulbach's *The Battle of the Huns*. Tchaikovsky also took
literary texts as his starting point in *Hamlet*, *Romeo and
Juliet*,and *Francesca da Rimini* (which has recently been made
the musical basis of a ballet). The next development of an
elastic form was geographical and one gets a series of posters
from many parts of the world—Smetana portrays Bohemia in
a series with the title *Ma Vlast* (my country), Borodin the Step-
pes of Central Asia (so named), Sibelius his own Finland in
Finlandia and more recently Respighi with his Roman pictures,
The Fountains of Rome, *The Pines of Rome*, and *A Roman Holiday*. Delius did the same for Paris in an orchestral nocturne.
Strauss, who seems to have a keen and almost scientific interest
in psychology, took the matter further and used his enormous
technical mastery for the delineation of minute subtleties, and
indeed abnormalities, of character. He began in 1888 with
a study of Don Juan, who was a libertine ' with a difference ',
who would " fain run the circle, immeasurably wide, of beautiful women's manifold charms . . . and would keep himself
fresh in the service of beauty ". *Macbeth* followed, then
Tod und Verklärung with a typically German transfiguration,
consisting of a treacly mixture of sentiment, metaphysics and
bombast. From the cheerful, extravagant and endearing rascal Till Eulenspiegel he turned to the philosophical mind in
Zarathustra, became an alienist in *Don Quixote*, perhaps the
most sympathetic of them all because of its compassionate
epilogue, and finally exposed the full unpleasantness of the

German character when it indulges in heroics in *Ein Helden-leben* (The Hero's Life—the hero's works of peace being, if you please, self-quotations from the works of Richard Strauss). The virtuosity of *Heldenleben* makes it a favourite piece for conductors and blinds the public to the fundamentally repellent character of the hero.

Tone poems on every conceivable kind of subject from Celtic folk-lore to modern industrialism—the Russians go so far as to depict steel foundries and power stations in music—would suggest that composers, like the satirist, take for their motto *humani nihil a me alienum puto* and find the rich spectacle of human life stimulating to the creation of illustrative music. The tendency is perhaps to keep the symphonic poem on smaller lines than those of the symphony. The last symphonic poem to be written on the heroic scale was Elgar's *Falstaff*, whose complexity, however rewarding to study, is inevitably a little bewildering in the fleeting conditions of concert performance. The most recent essay in a form which depends structurally upon the use of Wagnerian *Leitmotiven* or ' guiding themes ' is the pert neo-Aesopian fable of *Peter and the Wolf* in which Prokofiev uses the speaking voice for his narrative, which is thereupon closely illustrated in aptly entertaining music.

There was a tendency at one time to deprecate programme music as inferior to absolute music and to place all illustrative works in a class below symphonies. If the symphony is reserved for the expression of lofty aspiration or of searching logical thought it follows that works which seek to entertain are in another, a different and in a sense a lower category. But there is really nothing derogatory in writing or listening to descriptive music. Composers always have done it and they always will. Indeed they cannot help it, any more than we can fail to be pleased and entertained by it. For in virtue of the universal symbolizing powers of the human mind, of which I have already written, the auditor has little difficulty in translating back the composer's symbols into their ' meaning '. Music cannot make statements of precise fact, and if it sounds sad the hearer does not always know whether it is an unhappy love affair or a toothache that has caused the depression of spirits. But actually one can tell extraordinarily well what is going on in a musical narrative—musical symbols are widely intelligible, they are not a private language of composers. Take a case of a flowing melody in 12/8 time; it is not convention that calls this a pastorale; that is the musical imagery which the mind uses to convey the impression of rustic peace; it is a symbol not a conventional sign. The listener recognizes the composer's meaning without thinking twice about it and to his musical pleasure, in fact, is added the Aristotelian pleasure of ἀναγνώρισις, dramatic recognition. There will never be any shortage of programme music or of audiences for it.

Similarly, however difficult is their defence on strict æsthetic principles, operatic excerpts have been in the past, still are and apparently always will be, a feature of orchestral programmes. A hundred years ago even the Philharmonic Society regularly admitted the pot-pourri of operatic melodies to an equal place with chamber music and orchestral symphonies in its concert schemes. The motives for their inclusion are three, of which the first is a desire to make the acquaintance of any new style of composition, or of any new composer of powerful personality for which, as so often happens in this country, there is no pro- vision in the theatre. Wagner came to England and conducted concerts of his music in the fifties and the seventies of last cen- tury, and a recent parallel is the production by the B.B.C. of Berg's *Wozzeck* and Hindemith's *Mathis the Painter* in concert form as well as the inclusion of excerpts from those works in an ordinary miscellaneous programme. The second inducement is the opposite to the first—a desire to hear again what is already familiar and is known to give pleasure. A pot-pourri from Gounod's *Faust* will still please a seaside audience on a Saturday night. The third justification of transposing operatic music from the stage to the platform applies only to a country like England which is not operatically minded. Here a large part of the musical public is offended by operatic convention, due no doubt in part to its ignorance of the operatic repertory and unfamiliarity with dramatic music in general. But whatever the cause, prejudice against opera is a force to be reckoned with. When a star of the first magnitude like Wagner floats into the firmament and music lovers have no other means of enjoying music that is unlike anything else ever written, they will gladly listen to excerpts and be quite unperturbed by the late Sir Donald Tovey's designation of them as 'bleeding chunks'. Furthermore Wagner's later operas are not readily accessible to

English opera-goers, and if one is to make any close acquaintance with the music of *The Ring* the concert-hall offers a place for such first-hand study. Hence the all-Wagner concert, such as the London Symphony Orchestra included regularly once a season in its series, and such as Sir Henry Wood assigns to Monday nights during the Proms.

The æsthetic objections are that chunks hacked out of a more than usually continuous tissue—and one of Wagner's points in the æsthetic of music-drama is that the tissue is continuous, and not divided up into set pieces as in Mozart and heroic Italian opera—are bound to bleed, in spite of the transference of voice parts to violins, the composition of innocuous joins and the addition of final cadences. In the case of the pot-pourri the objection is really one of form. The keys of the various arias may find themselves in incongruous juxtaposition and no sort of unity of tonality is possible in a selection of favourite extracts from a popular opera. In Wagner the formal objection, though still valid, is less potent in that Wagner's texture is symphonic—again it was part of his creed to apply symphonic methods of development to dramatic music. Several of the most familiar excerpts like the " Ride of the Valkyries ", " Forest Murmurs ", and " Siegfried's Funeral March " are fairly self-subsistent episodes in the drama which can be detached from their context without undue violence. In the case of the Prelude and Liebestod from *Tristan* the organic connexion binding this combination of the beginning and the end of a huge opera is close. It has been well said that the whole of *Tristan* develops from the opening bars of the Prelude. The Liebestod is the crown and fulfilment of a long development through three acts. The two selections which fit so well together are therefore Prologue and Epilogue, and together summarize in a compressed form the whole opera. Certainly they are logical and coherent.

Operatic music has its special attractions—the broad sweeping melody of Italian arias, the vivid pictorial quality of Wagner's nature tone-poems, the dramatic point and excitement inherent in music for the stage. These things make an immediate appeal to an audience which may not be sensitive to niceties of construction, though, however unconscious it may be of the reasons for it, the lay mind draws a greater satisfaction from what is well made than from something less coherent. But in the operatic extract the more vivid pleasures outweigh the un-realized subtleties of logical unity.

A similar question arises from the performance of transcriptions of music that is composed for one medium, such as the piano or organ, transferred to another such as the orchestra. There are good reasons against any such procedure and the purist is never quite happy when he hears even the most discreet adaptation of the works of Bach to a modern full orchestra. It is like the æsthetic objection to the 'arrangement' of a folk-song. The folk-song is melody in its purest form, why then adulterate it with a quite unnecessary accompaniment? The answer is : Why indeed ? except that everyone, even the strictest folk-musician, cannot refrain from doing it. The folk-song is a perfect work of art in itself, but it is also capable of being the raw material of a secondary work of art derived from it. Similarly, a Prelude and Fugue by Bach for the organ is complete, self-sufficient, and, if you will, perfect, as it is. But if Elgar transcribes it boldly for full orchestra, it becomes another work of art, secondary to and derived from the original but yielding a new satisfaction. Like everything else in art the actual transcription may be good or bad and each instance must be judged on its merits. The general principle of judgment will be like that of deciding what is a good folk-song arrangement. If it is done with love by one who knows, by one who has thoroughly absorbed the style of the original and can refrain from the itch 'to make something of it', then a good transcription may emerge. Bach himself, it may be recalled, was an assiduous transcriber of his own music.

There are cases which require even less defence. A certain amount of music exists which was composed for instruments now obsolete, such as the lute. A good deal of music lies embedded in forgotten plays and operas, Purcell's incidental music and Handel's Italian operas for instance. Some of such music can be salved by suitable adaptation and makes a welcome variety in the standard repertory. A few cases exist where sheer delight in manipulating the orchestral box of tricks and the sheer skill with which it is done delight one by the sheer impertinence of the transcription. On the other hand there are some dreadful examples of thickening and inflation and noise ; it is for example a solecism to add the organ at the climax to a work composed for the organ and so to confuse the whole basis of the transcription.

It is extraordinary, or would be if it was not inherent in the nature of music itself to betray the hand of the artist, how the personality of the transcriber gets into the sound-texture of the transcription. Bach transcribed by Wood sounds heavily romantic, like Wagner and Tchaikovsky; Bach transcribed by Elgar sounds magniloquent; Bach transcribed by Walton gives off electric sparks. A curious case is Ravel's transcription of Moussorgsky's suite for piano, *Pictures at an Exhibition*. This must be one of the best transcriptions ever made. Nothing seems to have been added or lost—it is an exact translation from one medium into another. Ravel, though a brilliant and judicious manipulator of the orchestra, was in the habit of writing his own works first for the piano and then translating them into orchestral terms, unlike Beethoven who said he always heard a particular melody on the instrument to which it belonged, and unlike most other composers who may certainly jot down their ideas in short score but probably have a pretty good idea of how they intend to dispose them in full score. Ravel's practice with his own works enabled him to perform a similar service for Moussorgsky without offence.

Overtures, suites from ballet music, excerpts from operas, transcriptions from the keyboard (or other media), these and all such borrowings add spice to the repertory. Programme music in its manifold manifestations, and with its wide range of subjects, may be regarded as the sweets of a meal.

CHAPTER IX

CONDUCTING AND CONDUCTORS

CONDUCTORS have during the past generation usurped the place of singers in popular esteem; as personalities they have become more interesting than the prima donnas. This is in itself significant of the shift of public taste towards orchestral music at the expense of opera, oratorio and the ballad concert. A singer gifted with a beautiful voice becomes willy-nilly the focus of attention; we all admire a display of skill, and virtuosity in any accomplishment commands admiration and applause. The conductor has no power of immediate appeal equivalent to the direct fascination of the human voice, but as the controller of the many-voiced orchestra he appears like a magician with miraculous powers. We abase ourselves before one whose nod, nay, whose flicker of an eyelid, can call forth the thunder and whose little finger can still the storm. His prestige is enormous. He works through prestige-suggestion and when a hundred self-willed artists are subdued to the minutest execution of his will, we of the audience feel a similar subservience overflowing from orchestra to us—so long at any rate as we are not infuriated at his misinterpretations of a favourite work. We are impressed by his power—and a conductor must be an impressive person, whether he impresses by the spiritual equivalent of a massive forehead, a flashing eye or an exuberant crop of hair. I once heard Mr. Winston Churchill say that he envied a conductor his autocratic powers, not so much because they were autocratic, as because of the immediacy, the subtlety and the magnitude of the response to his smallest gesture. Mr. Churchill has since shown that his observation of the ways of orchestral conductors has not been wasted; he realizes that the conductor does not blow his own trombone or scratch his own double-bass; he gives the word and a harmonious ministry corporately functions. Individual and corporate effort are complementary; a War Premier, like an orchestral conductor, depends on the consent of his colleagues, but he provides the initiative and the direction for the team. It is because the public has realised that an orchestra of capable players is like a Cabinet of good men that they accord to a conductor an adulation, which may seem excessive to critics of more sober and sceptical temper, for making all the difference between a lively and a deadly symphony, as a Prime Minister makes all the difference between a policy of vigour and a policy of drift.

The psychology of an orchestra is not so incalculable as that of a boat-race crew, but it is of a more sensitive kind than could survive in the hurly-burly of politics. The tonal balance of an orchestral ensemble, fluctuating minutely from moment to moment, involves a degree of co-operation and mutual adjustment comparable to that of a game of football. Now any sort of team that has developed a corporate spirit develops also sensitiveness to suggestion ; a herd of animals (or men) in a panic is in this respect like a disciplined company of soldiers ; response to suggestion is instantaneous in both, and enormous power is engendered and released by their action in combination. The difference between these two cases of mass action is that one is uncontrolled and the other is orderly. The orchestra is even more purposive in its corporate activity than a company of men obedient to orders ; it has actually cultivated its sensibility to suggestion. A conductor, then, unable perhaps to communicate by language with the players in an orchestra which he is conducting in a foreign country, may yet secure the results he desires by expressive gestures. Conducting in fact is making gestures with a little stick. And it works by suggestion.

Many musicians have not this power of suggestion, not from lack of knowledge or lack of authority but from an insufficient gregariousness and deficiency of a certain type of public self-confidence. A scholar for instance with a fierce mind (and scholars are extremely fierce) but a mild eye may be unable to cope with the herd behaviour of an orchestra—still less with a choir. Schumann was a case of a man of determination and abundant musical knowledge, though a poet rather than a scholar, who had no grip on a public assembly and as a conductor was a failure. Sir Arnold Bax, who is possessed of an uncanny skill with a score, a composer whose music and temperament have some affinity with Schumann's, has always refused utterly to take a baton in hand and conduct any of his works. At the other extreme is a sergeant-major who can make the band play though he has little knowledge and less art, but he has the herd mind, not the submissive but the assertive herd mind. For in this matter of prestige-suggestion two complementary qualities are involved—what McDougall called positive and negative self-feeling. The conductor when he is conducting, must be dominant, the orchestra, when it is playing, must be submissive. The conductor therefore must be capable of positive self-feeling in the face of the public. He had in fact better not be shy. Shyness is sometimes regarded as a moral virtue—certainly it is sometimes a sign of modesty—but it is generally a public nuisance, and the public likes public behaviour from a public man. This does not mean that the conductor must seek publicity or in private life be anything but unselfish, but it does mean that he must be sufficiently gregarious to be a part, and a leading part, of a crowd.

The other necessary element in a conductor's equipment is all-round musicianship. All-round means double-sided. The conductor must be a musician in the same sense that a Doctor of Music is a musician, and also a musician in the sense that a performing artist, such as a pianist or a singer, is a musician. The first kind of musical knowledge is sometimes called by the unilluminating name of theory; what it comprises is harmony, counterpoint, analysis, the ability to read a score (with all its implications of transposing instruments) and a great deal of detailed knowledge of the working of the instruments under his command. The other ability is all that is comprised in the word ' interpretation '. It is this part of a conductor's functions that is most obvious to the public, but the two sides, the technical and the imaginative, are not divorced. Hermann Scherchen's *Handbook of Conducting* prescribes a thorough grounding in theoretical and practical musicianship—the latter including what is now known in this country as aural training, *i.e.* an ability to analyse a congeries of sounds presented to the ear either as a melody or as a chord or as a piece of counterpoint in several parts ; in addition to that he prescribes a general culture and a historical knowledge of cultural movements. This is more important than is generally realized, for conductors, like other eminent musicians, often show themselves defective in a sense of style. The conductor, says Scherchen, " must be capable of distingushing between the style of a period, and the style of the man, between general conventions and individual conventions ". Some are incapable of distinguishing the styles of different periods, as is shown by the transcriptions and re-arrangements one hears of works by Bach and Handel, which are often made to sound post-Wagnerian. Like the pianist who fails to observe any stylistic difference between Scarlatti and Schumann, or as in one eminent example between Beethoven's three periods, some conductors approach all music as ' just music ' and trust to their native sensibility to secure a right interpretation. It cannot be done. Knowledge is necessary as well as imagination.

When this general knowledge has been acquired, Scherchen would allow his student to learn clear gestures with a stick and to come to the details of a score, which he says must be memorized. Memorizing does not mean merely knowing the notes, so that the harmony and the tune and the bass can be checked as correct, but having a detailed knowledge of every individual part. It is doubtful whether many conductors who conduct from memory could whistle the second clarinet part 22 bars after letter B in the score. Toscanini, however, we gather from Mr. Bernard Shore's illuminating revelation of famous conductors in their workshops, has got this close knowledge of his scores, driven thereto perhaps by the shortness of his sight and the consequent uselessness to him of a score at rehearsal. Scherchen then tackles with a wealth of examples the fine details of interpretation : up bow or down bow in such a passage of Beethoven's violin concerto, the varying rates of crescendo of the different wood-wind instruments in a passage from the Prelude to *Tristan* owing to the different power of flutes, oboes, clarinets in their several registers, double-tonguing with the right accents for the brass in *Till Eulenspiegel*, the correct adjustments in tone between side drum, cymbals and bass drum in Stravinsky. Such details have to be fitted into the conductor's broad general conception of the work in hand.

This kind of detailed work has recently been made available for the general reader's inspection at close quarters in Mr. Shore's unusual and interesting book, *The Orchestra Speaks*, already mentioned. Here we are shown the best-known conductors —Weingartner, Walter, Furtwängler are the most conspicuous absentees—engaged in the actual business of rehearsal. Here it is not a matter of suggestion but of definite instruction. The conductor builds up his imaginative conception of the work as a whole by the precise placing of each expressive stroke. Suggestion is a process of emotional contagion, instruction is a communication of knowledge. Both are necessary to the realization of any highly wrought interpretation. Some conductors, notably Mengelberg and Sir Henry Wood, go to the length of having their own sets of carefully marked parts so that the facts of the music, such as phrasing and dynamic changes, may be in front of the player and so to that extent relieve the conductor's hands of interpretative business. But there are many occasions in the concert world when no rehearsal is possible at all and the conductor has to realize his ideas from the score and parts provided, without the opportunity of talking to the orchestra. General conception and expressive detail have both to be conveyed by significant gesture. It was primarily to meet this case—unfortunately of far too frequent occurrence in London concerts after the last war and still sometimes inevitable in the arduous conditions of the Proms— that stick technique has been clarified and codified.

It was enough for a conductor like Richter to beat time, and indicate where the melody lay—the two requirements of a conductor specified by Wagner, who, whether he realized it or not, really wrought a revolution in conducting and brought about the rise of the modern virtuoso. No need for Richter to have a light and delicately balanced baton. His beat was decisive ; he could impart his musicianship to his regular orchestras at Bayreuth, Covent Garden, and the Hallé at Manchester in vigorous German or broken English ; and his sympathies were not unduly circumscribed,—though he once told a Hallé subscriber that there was no French music—since he successfully launched Elgar's greatest works upon the world. But as the suggestibility of the orchestra has increased, so have the means of suggestion become more refined. Too refined, one sometimes thinks, when an orchestra miraculously manages to make a clean start to some clear-cut phrase like the opening of the Fifth Symphony with no more than a rattle of linen cuffs. It has come to be considered unprofessional to give any ' beats for nothing ' which would clearly establish the tempo in such cases, though Koussevitsky, according to Mr Shore, in his search for perfection of execution does not despise introductory beats. Mr. Shore's comment is that " it certainly ensures confidence in setting a new tempo " in a difficult opening like that of the scherzo of the Eroica. Of course it does.

The new stick technique of conducting, the invention of Artur Nikisch, was first formulated in English by Adrian Boult in a handbook compact of general principles and useful dodges. Of general principles an example is the instruction to keep the stick swinging if you want to secure a firm rhythm. A jerky movement which aims at marking the rhythm defeats its own object. The swing suggests the underlying rhythm; crisp articulation is secured by seeing that the stick reaches its extreme positions at the appointed moments with a double movement which Boult calls the 'click', then the player knows, without having to stop to think or count or watch, precisely when the second, the third or the fourth beat is reached and still more infallibly when the first beats come. Of dodges the most useful was the change introduced in beating the second beat of a bar of three time. The old method was to beat three time and four time alike ; beat a down beat for one, swing to the left for two, over to the right for three in a bar of four time or up for three in a bar of three time. Now in order to prevent any momentary confusion in a player's mind as to the time of what he is playing, the second beat is beaten to the left in square time, to the right in triple.

The purpose of the stick is greater visibility and greater nuance than can be indicated over the distance involved by the hand alone. Boult insists that the stick is an extra limb whose function is the precise articulation of musical meaning. Sir Henry Wood advocates painting the baton white so as still further to ensure its being seen by all—for the stick has to be seen out of the corner of the eye without being directly looked at. Players have to keep their eyes on their music and cannot look at the conductor, as choralists are implored to do. Anything therefore that makes for visibility without looking is to be adopted. White paint is not however a universal prescription. Dr. Sargent conducts across the front of his body, which is to say in front of his white waistcoat and white dress shirt. He directs the point of his stick across himself towards his first violins, so he does not paint his sticks. Some of his imitators even make the mistake of keeping still the point of the stick while sawing the handle end up and down in front of their waistcoats. Their black sleeves are certainly visible, but there is not much nuance in a black cuff and a closed fist. Sir Henry Wood's method is to conduct well in front of him so that his white stick moves in his right hand against his black coat. Boult's principle is similar : the point of the stick is directed in front. A half turn of the body can be made if the first violins want special attention. The point of the stick, then, is the business end and it is clear that quite minute movements can be made clearly visible by the travel of this long extra arm of the body and the greatest precision obtained. It is therefore a complete fallacy to do what many conductors do when they come to a passage or a movement of special delicacy—put the stick down and conduct with the open hand. I have seen a conductor attempt to start the tricky 12/8 rhythm of the Pastoral Symphony of Bach's *Christmas Oratorio* with a ripple along the middle three fingers of the two hands like that of an Oriental dancer. It did not work ; there was neither start nor rhythm. At one time Sir Thomas Beecham, who commands a wealth of spontaneous pantomimic gesture, used to conduct without a stick, but he has long given up the practice, because one of his chief technical aims is the combination of delicacy and precision. The point of the stick is the ideal medium for minute and precise indications of speed, attack and the finer gradations of tone.

One other requirement of a conductor is a fine ear. It is not generally realized that musical endowment is not one gift of nature but half a dozen and no one musician, however gifted, has them all in supreme measure. Great acuity of ear which is usually regarded as *the* musical gift *par excellence* does not necessarily accompany the imagination of the composer, the fine nervous control of the instrumentalist, or the dramatic sense of the singer. The only musician who really *must* have a sharp ear is the string player. It is a great advantage to a conductor to have one, though it will not help him for instance to comprehend the vast implications, musical and philosophical, of Wagner's *The Ring*, if he is an operatic conductor in a German theatre. But ideally a conductor should be able to stop a choir and orchestra in a fortissimo passage and say : ' Third horn, you played your third quaver a quarter of a tone too sharp. Take care there next time.' Stanford, who was a great, though not a virtuoso conductor, had this sort of ear. There is a story told of him attending a rehearsal of a new work by one of his pupils, who though a first-rate musician, was making rather heavy weather of the unaccustomed job of directing an orchestra and choir through unfamiliar music. In a resonant empty hall, it all sounded confused. Stanford who had only a vocal score, called out " See what that second oboe is playing, me bhoy," and so began the process of restoring order. On the other hand there is the story of another conductor, who has specialized in modern works, playing a certain work of Stravinsky for several years before someone else discovered that the trumpets had ten bars left out of their parts and had always come in that much too early without being spotted. In these days of technically well-equipped players, conductors do not have to bother so much about note perfection, but an acute ear is of value in insisting on true intonation. Sir Henry Wood has always been strict on fine tuning, even going so far, according to Mr. Shore, as to have his wind instruments tune at odds with the strings, so as to allow for the change of temperature which playing on them in a warm hall will make in their pitch.

The qualifications for the conductor then are a good ear, wide and deep musicianship, a commanding personality based either on personal magnetism or the distinction that comes from knowledge, and the artistic imagination which is the personal contribution that every performing musician brings to his art.

Conductors have an influence upon the sheer tone quality produced by the orchestra they conduct. It has been observed already that transcribers of other men's work tinge their scores with their own aural predilections, even if they use the same range of colours. So do conductors. Weingartner tends to produce great clarity combined with depths of tone, Wood prefers a fully saturated and rather thick tone, American conductors like Stokowski and Koussevitsky deliver their music with great surface brilliance. Boult is interested rather in the line and the dynamics than in the colour of a score, and Beecham with the possibility of a quicksilver and iridescent flash.

Of the many traits that distinguish Beecham's work from that of any other living conductor, his acute sensibility to tone is the chief. It is axiomatic that tone should be good : we judge singers primarily by their quality of voice and withold our final meed of praise from any pianist or singer whose tone is considered defective, no matter by what other merits it is offset. Nevertheless the necessity for beautiful tone is taken for granted rather than closely studied. With Beecham sheer saturation of sound, a unique iridescence of colour and an all-enveloping lyricism of quality are the first essentials of an orchestra. And whether they come from verbal instruction and hard work or by sheer contagion from the incessant singing in which he encourages his players, the outcome in the orchestra which he has created and trained, the London Philharmonic, is a tonal palette possessed by no other orchestra and possibly never realized before. This over-riding lyricism affects everything he touches : it somewhat reduces the epic scale of his *Ring*, for instance, and makes his *Lohengrin* more opera than music drama (to its improvement). It mollifies the stern element in Beethoven, and it thaws the northern starkness of Sibelius. I recall two symphonies at a Leeds Festival which were overwhelmingly beautiful but seemed to me wrong : Beethoven's Seventh and Sibelius's Second sounded like the products of Italy—warm, sunny, and in fact too lyrical. Interpretation, that is, is influenced both for good and towards stylistic error by this consuming and probably unconscious passion for such subtlety, sensuousness and wizardry of tone as has never occurred to anyone else to dream of. The gain is greater than the loss. Think, for instance, of Mendelssohn's *Hebrides* Overture, which, until Beecham played it, was always a greyish seascape ; Beecham moved it south and to high summer. By sheer sensuousness of tone he makes Delius comprehensible. (There is a little more to it than that, since Delius was incapable of phrasing his own music, and Beecham has had to do it for him). But it was Beecham who discovered wherein lay the basic essence of Delius's languid harmony, which is probably in the main a matter of chording, *i.e.* spreading the relative intensities of the components of a chord across the gamut in the right proportions.

What tone quality is to Beecham, architecture is to Boult, though possibly Boult's ideal is held as a more conscious artistic faith than is Beecham's instinctive drive towards the sensuous side of the art. If Beecham aims at building you a golden castle in the air, a castle, mark, which for the time you are living inside, not one you are looking at from outside, Boult rather aims at projecting for you as on a screen the magnificent constructions of the works of the masters. Boult's preoccupation with the formal aspects of music is linked with his attitude to the composer whose faithful servant he aims at being. His concern is that you in the audience should hear the symphony as Brahms, the composer, conceived it, in so far as he, the conductor, can bring it to life for you without distorting it through the medium of his own personality.   He has his own convictions, as any artist must have who is to present a work of art as a living organism and not as a dead demonstration of a scientific fact—the slow tempo at which he takes the " Sanctus " of the *B minor Mass* is the example that first occurs to me of a personal reading.   He has certain favourite works which he plays supremely well—Brahms's fourth symphony, Schubert's C major symphony, Ravel's *Daphnis et Chloe* suites, and Elgar's second symphony, a fairly varied selection of personal favourites, but in general his tastes are, apart from English choral music, which has always been a substantial interest in his career, mainly for the German classics.   This soundness on the classics is with him a good basis for soundness elsewhere, and of all living conductors in his class he is the safest for giving a sound, and therefore intelligible, performance of a modern work of any school whatsoever.   His performances of modern English works go beyond soundness and intelligibility ; they speak with conviction ; and he has done more for British composers than anyone except Sir Henry Wood.

If sheer catholicity of taste and an open mind towards old and new is the quality most in demand of a conductor, then the palm must be given to Sir Henry Wood.   We have all learned from him.   Most of us have learned our repertory from him. A vast number of orchestral players have been trained by him, and still to-day the students of the Royal Academy of Music have the advantage of learning their orchestral behaviour at his experienced hands.   The wider public is more likely to have learned from him than from anyone else what orchestral music is.   Forty-seven years of Promenade Concerts have introduced all sorts and conditions of music to all sorts and conditions of men, and during the ten years or so that the Proms were broadcast people in the remotest parts of Britain, who had never been to Queen's Hall and were never likely to go there, got to know Sir Henry Wood and his music.   He is in fact a national character.

A few years ago he celebrated his jubilee as a conductor. The whole of his long professional life has been devoted to conducting, although he played the organ as a boy and still teaches singing.   He has done many other things besides Proms. He has for instance played a large part in provincial music, as well as taking his share in London symphony concerts.   He has always kept an open mind, and to this day will readily learn a new score.   He has himself advanced with the movement of taste which he has helped to create.   This should never be forgotten by those who themselves outgrow and criticize some of his interpretations.   His omnivorous catholicity has done much to make known not only the classics and the romantics, but also the moderns to one generation after another of music lovers.   He was a pioneer of Tchaikovsky and he introduced Sibelius to London long before the present vogue began, and other Slavs, such as the Czechs for whom his coadjutor, Mrs. Rosa Newmarch, could speak, were congenial to him with their bright colours and strong rhythms.   It is the unflagging gusto that goes with this undiminished pleasure in exuberance that has kept Wood young, and it is what endears him to his public. More sophisticated tastes miss in his work fine shades of expression and find his permanently broad outlines and bold effects apt to be oppressive.   But it is true that he has captured for music his hundreds of thousands of lay listeners ; his vitality is invincible and his control unshakeable—no matter what mischief a soloist may be up to.

Another conductor conspicuous for versatility and a catholic taste is Dr. Malcolm Sargent.   If there is a job to be done from a festival performance of the *B minor Mass* to a Saturday night Gilbert and Sullivan opera, from training a students' orchestra to mingling instruction with entertainment for an audience of children, from accompanying Schnabel in a concerto for a gramophone record to steering an orchestra at short notice through a new work, Malcolm Sargent is the man to do it.   He owes his success, meteoric in the brilliance of its rise and like a planet in the steadiness of its progress, not merely to this resourcefulness of mind, and the quickness of his grasp alike of a situation and a score, but also to his capacity for work, which led a year or two ago to overwork and break-down.   He thinks easily and swiftly in musical terms.   He has ideas about other things too which he allows to fertilize his music, though here his nimble mind sometimes runs away with him on the surface of the subject.   A lively wit, genial temper, sufficient ambition, mastery of his craft, and an almost incredible faculty for getting and spending energy brought Sargent to the fore as one of the most useful and able conductors of the day.   Would these very

qualities preclude him from the ranks of the really great inter-
preters ?   The respite of his long illness not only conserved
his energies but consolidated his powers and opened up great
possibilities.   There are works which make a strong personal
appeal to him and in which he gets behind the notes to the
meaning.   I recall a performance of Dvorak's New World
Symphony which was given with a classical balance and purity
quite beyond the general animation and textual accuracy which
Sargent can be relied on to give.   Here there was a personal
conviction based on concentrated study of a work which one
might have expected to make only a hackneyed appeal to a versatile conductor.   It had a beautiful transparency, an unusual
regard for delicacy of instrumental colouring and an architectural poise that made the spontaneity of its feelings more
rather than less immediate for being held precisely within the
formal scheme of the work.

No conductor can afford to circumscribe his repertory unduly
by personal predilection, but some are more limited by their
own taste than others.   This defect, if so it can be called, has its
obverse, which is special excellence in the interpretation of congenial music.   Sir Landon Ronald was a conductor of superb
musicianship and technical mastery of an orchestra but at the
end of his career as a conductor, at any rate, he confined himself
to works for which he felt a special sympathy.   As an interpreter of Elgar he stood unequalled by any one except the composer himself.

Toscanini is a conductor who built up his great reputation
in opera but has in his later years done a good deal of concert
work and shown as a writer in Grove declares " that his tastes
know no limitation.   His interpretations of German music are
as finished and distinguished as his reading of Verdi or Debussy."
But I cannot coax myself into agreement with the general ver-
dict in England that his interpretations have final authority.
He is without question a supreme musician and his fidelity to
his scores gives some warrant for the common view that once
you have heard his readings, you have heard the composer's
own definitive view of the work.   But this is claiming too much
for anyone and I find certain limitations of national temperament affect his views of German works.   The *Meistersinger*
overture for instance in his hands ceases to be bourgeois and
provincial, and becomes a pageant of Florentine nobles.   His

nervous energy is tremendous but sometimes overdrives a way-ward work like Elgar's *Introduction and Allegro*. He naturally gets nearer to the spirit of Verdi's *Requiem* than of Brahms's, but with the universal spirit of Beethoven he is in complete accord ; his dynamism matches the composer's and his perfor-mance of Beethoven's symphonies has become canonical.

Another conductor with a national bias is Albert Coates, who is half Russian by blood—his mother was a Russian who married a Yorkshireman—and more than half Russian by tem-perament. He first came into prominence in England immedi-ately after the last war on the crest of the wave of enthusiasm for Russian art that followed in the wake of Diaghilev's Russian Ballet. Scriabin in particular had his vogue then (as never since) and Coates is a specialist in Scriabin, whose music he plays with enthusiasm and conviction. When after the Revo-lution Coates returned to England his specialist knowledge of all the Russians, both the nationalists which sounded exotic to western ears and the Moscow school of Europeanizers, commended him, ironically enough, to the anti-Bolshevik Eng-lish public, but his Brahms did not go down quite so well. Latterly he has only conducted in England intermittently. English taste is firmly based on the German classics, and Coates's interpretations do not run on classical lines, nor in spite of his cosmopolitan experience does his mind move naturally in Teu-tonic grooves. With the passing of the Russian fever, his special qualifications lost some of their power. But his all-round musicianship and the comprehensiveness with which he will embrace all music in his wide grasp has ensured that he turns up at Queen's Hall, at Covent Garden, in Yorkshire, or in a Russian programme at a seaside festival. It will take more than a change of fashion to remove so massive a figure from English musical life.

Ireland gave to Hamilton Harty the same sort of emotional bias from the point of view of interpretation as Russia gives to Coates. An Irishman with a warm temperament and lively wit, the late Sir Hamilton Harty was musically a thorough-going romantic, alike in his compositions and in his predilec-tions as a conductor. He was an enthusiast for Berlioz and was in natural sympathy with the acute mind, delicate fancy and soaring exuberance of that erratic Frenchman. Yet his own spontaneous and emotional response to it, as equally to Wagner and any other romantic, never upset the control of his direction. He communicated his lively feelings to the orchestra by natural magnetism and facial expression not by frantic gestures, for he had an exceptionally quiet manner on the platform. His sympathies were by no means limited to the romantic period. Handel fired him to re-score the Water Music ; Constant Lambert and William Walton both had first performances of important works at his hands. He made an immediate success both of *Rio Grande* and of Walton's symphony and he introduced Shostakovitch to an English audience. He was an ideal accompanist of a concerto. He came to the rostrum from the organ loft via the piano. He was indeed a prince of piano accompanists, and his experience in this field left its mark on his work as a conductor—quick sympathy, warmth of tone, absence of show and fuss and great nimbleness of musicianship were some of the valuable qualities thus transferred from the one sphere to the other. He had a delicate ear for tone colour and a sensitive perception of what is apt, so that his transcriptions, of which the most recent is a delightful suite made up out of the piano works of John Field, are apposite renderings of the originals. In his own compositions he was inclined to a heavier laying on of colour to accord with the unashamed and by now, it must be confessed, somewhat outmoded romanticism of his original work. It will easily be understood that his particular blend of qualities issued in an unforced charm ; Harty commended music to you, and his handling of the players in the orchestra, one gathers from Mr. Shore, was equally persuasive.

Of the international figures Weingartner had the largest and most stable following in England. A product of the ripest period of romanticism—he belonged to the circle of Liszt— he is now esteemed as the supreme exponent of the German classics, especially Beethoven and Brahms. His quiet manner on the platform and restrained gestures secured readings that were mellow but not lacking in force, of classical poise and the utmost transparency of texture. As a composer he has never realized his hopes, since his music is derivative. England has known little of his work as a conductor of opera but in 1939 he took charge of Wagner at Covent Garden to general satisfaction.

Furtwängler has never quite convinced English audiences of the supreme quality which the Germans ascribe to him. His performances with the Berlin Philharmonic Orchestra were marked by vivid contrasts of dynamics which English taste regarded as somewhat extravagant, even while it admired them as something which our own orchestras never produced. Technically it always seemed a miracle that his orchestra should respond with such miraculous precision to his curiously wavering stick. The onlooker could not make up his mind whether his head or his baton gave the effective sign, but effective it was, and the discipline of the orchestra was one of its most striking attributes. When he conducted the *Ring* at Covent Garden we got a better idea of the breadth of his vision, since he conceived it and interpreted it on an epic scale.

Fritz Busch, late of Dresden, but known in England only at Glyndebourne, and therefore a less familiar figure than his brother Adolf the violinist, has conducted no concerts here so that we have only the operas of Mozart wherewith to gauge his artistic quality. From his performances at Glyndebourne we know that he combines German thoroughness with lightness of touch. The playing under his hands comes up crisp, and his tempi seem inevitably right. He is a conductor of international eminence whose art we have yet to discover.

So too, though the remark applies with less force since we meet him on gramophone records, is Stokowski. Although he was largely English trained—at the Royal College of Music—his work with orchestra has been done wholly in America with the Philadelphia Symphony Orchestra. From his records one would judge that brilliance of tone and rhythmic energy were the predominant qualities of his musical style, but I once heard him conduct a performance of *Meistersinger* Overture under unusual circumstances. It was at the Jubilee of his old College in 1933 when he conducted unrehearsed an orchestra of ex-Royal College students. He played up the strings and subdued the wind and brought off an effect of razor-edged excitement.

Another conductor whom the Royal College has given to America is Eugene Goossens, whom we hear too rarely now in this country. Member of a famous and gifted family of musicians of British nationality but Flemish extraction, Goossens by birth, by environment, by training and by natural capacity is a musician to the finger tips which hold his baton. Those same fingers at one time held a violin bow, and they sometimes hold a pen, though his compositions win no very wide favour, being what critics describe as musicianly, and what others more bluntly pronounce as ' dry '.   They have many good qualities but lack heart.   It is possible to say the same of his interpretations, but the other good qualities make up for and conceal any deficiencies in this respect.   He is far too understanding a musician to take out of a fervent composer any of the warmth that is already there, even if he does not pump hot blood into the creations of his own mind.   His insistence on high technical standards, based on his own technical accomplishment and the importance attached to sheer brilliance of execution by the American public, gives distinction to whatever he touches.

This brief critical survey of some of the best-known conductors and their work does not aim at doing more than to show how the musical personality of the conductor emerges just as clearly in the handling of his human instrument as does the pianist's in his physical touch of the key or the violinist's in the stroke of his bow.   His control of the actual sound-producing medium is exercised indirectly and, as it were, across a gap, yet he can obtain instant response to his subtlest intentions. The rich expressive capacity of the orchestra as a corporate instrument of music is a neverfailing source of wonder, and it is not surprising that the desire to take control of one of man's most complex and potent creations fires the ambitions of most musicians, or that the exercise of such power goes to the head of many an aspirant.   To conduct an orchestra is to exercise the tyranny of one's dreams and the magic of the wizard—for what is a wizard but a man of knowledge and power ?   No wonder that the successful conductor who controls one of the most responsive vehicles of human thought and feeling is idolized by the public.   He must not play the tyrant, however, even though he may be a martinet.   He must submit himself to one who is greater than he, namely the composer whom it is his duty to serve.   And he must serve also the players whom he leads, for without them he is powerless.   But when a great conductor, great in humility as in knowledge, wisdom and art, plays a great symphony to a crowded audience of the initiated, then there is achieved an act of fellowship, such as no other art but the drama can accomplish, and a spiritual exaltation that goes beyond the theatre's tales of human passion.

APPENDIX I

GRAMOPHONE RECORDS

The enterprise of the various recording companies has put within the reach of any music lover the great bulk of the music mentioned in this book. He is more likely to find his choice of a domestic orchestral repertory limited by the inelasticity of his pocket than by inability to track down a record that he wants.

The present conditions of war no doubt seriously limit the resources that were available in peace time. Records made in Germany and marketed in Britain by Parlophone are in short supply and no accessions are now being made to the list. The English companies have revised their catalogues so that the buyer may not be able to obtain such works as never had a great popular demand and have in consequence been withdrawn during the present stringency of materials. I have not therefore thought it worth while to append any list of records as musical illustrations to my text, since it is liable at any moment from now onwards to be out of date in both directions : what once was available may have been withdrawn and the activities of the recording companies cannot be foreseen by the author of a general book like this.

Readers are more likely to have difficulty in forming an idea of what the early music of the embryonic orchestra sounded like than of anything subsequently composed. But a certain small amount of music played on old instruments has been recorded, notably by the Dolmetsch Family for Columbia. Viols, lutes and recorders, as well as the keyed instruments contemporary with them, can be heard on these records. Modern instruments can be heard in isolation on two specially devised H.M.V. records (C.1311 and 1312), on which strings, wood-wind, brass and percussion play characteristic passages.

Of eighteenth century concertos and concerti grossi there is an increasing supply available. Decca, for instance, has issued the complete set of Handel's twelve concerti grossi recorded by the Boyd Neel Orchestra. The Busch recordings of Bach's Brandenburg Concertos (Columbia) are outstanding. Unfortunately no wholly satisfactory performance of Bach's D minor concerto for two violins has yet appeared, although at least three attempts have been made by eminent violinists. There is a record of Corelli's Christmas Concerto by Parlophone.

In the matter of symphonies not all of Haydn's 104 or of Mozart's 49 are recorded. On the other hand a variety of interpretations of Beethoven's 9 are obtainable. Sir Thomas Beecham's records of Haydn and Mozart for Columbia may in general be recommended both for style of performance and smooth quality of recording. With less known works the gramophone is sometimes more generous than concert givers. Thus symphonies by Roussel, d'Indy and Prokofiev, which are seldom to be heard in public though they are on rare occasions broadcast by the B.B.C., have been recorded. The activities of the various " Societies " are important in this connection. Sibelius, for instance, has three of his symphonies in the general list of H.M.V. and four in the Sibelius Society's albums.

The chief solo concertos are well catered for, because eminent soloists naturally need them for their recorded performances. Thus, for instance, some particularly outstanding performances of violin concertos by Jascha Heifetz have recently given us new records of Beethoven's, Brahms's and Walton's concertos. More than one reading of the chief concertos are available and the companies' catalogues should be consulted.

To cater for the increased interest in ballet, more and more ballet music is being recorded and the H.M.V. catalogue has an entry which is a guide to the principal music from this source in the orchestral repertory. Overtures, tone poems and miscellaneous short pieces are legion, but can all be traced under their composers' names.

A word may be added as a warning to users of acoustic gramophones that some recent brilliant imports from U.S.A. are too heavily recorded for fibre needles, which often break down under the strain before a single side is played through. It would be presumptuous to advise gramophone users on a choice of machine or needles or to recommend one recording company rather than another. I do myself, however, prefer a good acoustic gramophone to any electrical machine which in my view always puts a veneer over the true tone. Further-more I do not think it is an advantage to be able to regulate brilliance of high and low registers by turning knobs, as it introduces an incalculable factor into the dynamics of the music. For fidelity of reproduction, therefore, I think the acoustic machine is preferable. On the other hand no trouble arises from needles with a radiogram, which, being two instruments in one, has the obvious advantage of convenience.

———

APPENDIX II

P. 14.   The use of four horns was anticipated, exceptionally, by Haydn in Symphony No. 31 for the 'Horn Signal' in D, and by Mozart in Symphonies K 130 and K 318 and in Divertimento K 131.

P. 71.   Verdi had been anticipated in the use of violoncellos alone in self-subsistent harmony by Rossini in the overture to *William Tell*.
  The full score of *Salome* has a footnote by Strauss, to the effect that these utterances of the double-bass represent the maddened pantings of the expectant Salome. As there are about twenty of these notes they would represent some fumbling on the exe-cutioner's part if one took them as literally representative of sword strokes. But the situation in the theatre is that John the Baptist is invisible in the 'cistern', one knows he is being despatched and one hears the filthy noises. Anyhow the effect is, as the composer intended, disgusting, whether it is body-lust or blood-lust that animates the phlegamatic contra-bass. Another example of the powers of darkness choosing a contra-bass as their instrument is the solo assigned to it by Verdi when Otello enters Desdemona's bedroom with murder in his heart.

P. 88   The tendency to begin a symphony with a slow introduction grew upon Haydn: of his twelve 'London' symphonies eleven have such slow introductions.

P. 104   Both of Brahms's Serenades, however, Op. 11 in D and Op. 16 in A, contain scherzos. Indeed, in Op. 11 there are two.

P. 116   Prokofiev returned to Russia about 1934 and brought out in Moscow the music to the satirical film *Lieutenant Kije*, which has been heard in London with a ballet and has become available on gramophone records. *Peter and the Wolf* was written for a children's concert in 1936.
  Shostakovitch has impressed his name more forcibly on the British public since this book was first published by his 'Lenin-grad' symphony, an immensely long work composed during the siege of Leningrad in the winter of 1941-2.

INDEX

Abraham, Gerald   109
Adam, Adolphe
    Giselle   138
Alexander, Samuel   91
Atonality   74

Bach, Carl Philip Emanuel   18, 20, 81, 93, 94, 135
Bach, Johann Christian   18, 20, 93, 96
Bach, Johann Sebastian   27, 104, 119, 146, 147, 151
    Orchestration   18, 19, 20, 41, 48, 122
    Brandenburg Concertos   17, 18, 121, 122, 123, 134, 165
       No. 1   16, 17, 123
       No. 2   44, 53, 54, 121
       No. 3   122
       No. 4   17, 37, 123
       No. 5   121, 122, 123
       No. 6   70, 122, 123
    Concertos for clavier and for violin   124, 127-8, 135
    Mass in B minor   14, 19, 157, 158
    Pastoral Symphony   154
    St. Matthew Passion   39, 43
    Suites   138
    Suite in B minor for flute   134
    Well-tempered Clavier   79
Barnett, J. F.   104
Barr, Herbert   54
Bartlett, Ethel   135
Bartok, Bela   110
Bax, Sir Arnold   81, 88, 149
    Symphonies   112-3
    Symphony No. 5   88
Beecham, Sir Thomas   5, 8, 10, 50, 106, 154, 155-6
Beethoven, Ludwig van   9, 48, 56, 58, 80, 81, 88, 92,
       95, 96, 99-102, 105, 112, 119,
       120, 147, 151, 160, 161
    Sonata-rondo   89, 97
    Andante favori   89
    Battle of Vittoria   61
    Concertos for piano
       No. 1 in C   129
       No. 2 in B flat   129
       No. 3 in C minor   125
       No. 4 in G   125-6, 129, 133
       No. 5 in E flat (Emperor)   24, 87, 126, 129
    Concerto for violin   60, 125, 131, 132, 151
    Concerto for violin, violoncello and piano   135
    Grosse Fuge   89
    Mass in D   14, 72
    Overtures
       Overture in C   9
       Egmont   39, 138
       King Stephen   9
       Leonora No. 3   139
       Ruins of Athens   9
    Prelude (op. 39)   79
    Prometheus   67

Beethoven, Ludwig van—*continued.*
    Sonata, ' Waldstein '   89
    String quartets   13
    Symphonies
        No. 1 in C   23, 88, 100
        No. 2 in D   88, 100
        No. 3 in E flat (Eroica)   14, 27, 51, 88, 100,101, 152
        No. 4 in B flat   22, 60, 85-7, 88, 100, 101
        No. 5 in C minor   14, 48, 82, 83, 88, 100, 101,
                            106, 152
        No. 6 in F (Pastoral)   39, 96, 102, 104, 106, 112, 141
        No. 7 in A   88, 100, 101, 156
        No. 8 in F   60, 100, 102
        No. 9 in D minor (Choral) 14, 15, 23, 44, 48, 51, 52, 60,
                            63, 90, 100, 101, 103
Benedict, Julius   11
Bennett, William Sterndale   11
Berg, Alban   *Wozzeck*   144
Bériot, C. A. de   120
Berkeley, Lennox   *Introduction and Allegro*   135
Berlin Philharmonic Orchestra   3, 4, 60, 161   [142, 160
Berlioz, Hector   15, 18, 24, 25, 26, 56, 58, 92, 108,
        Carnaval Romain   43
        Damnation de Faust, La   67
        Fantastic Symphony   43, 60, 104, 106-7
        Harold in Italy   24, 71
        Requiem Mass   25, 60
        Romeo and Juliet   15, 63
        Treatise on Instrumentation 24, 25, 56
        Troyens, Les   63
Bishop, Sir Henry   9
Bizet, Georges
        L'Arlésienne   47, 62
        Carmen   64
Bliss, Arthur   110, 113
        Checkmate   139,
        Concerto for Two Pianos 135
        Music for Strings   71, 123
Blom, Eric   99
Boehm, Theobald   39, 45
Borodin, Alexander
        Steppes of Central Asia 142
        Symphony in B minor 109
Boston Symphony Orchestra   3
Boughton, Rutland   41
Boult, Sir Adrian   5, 105, 153, 154, 155, 156-7
Bournemouth Municipal Orchestra   6, 8, 60
Brahms, Johannes   14, 24, 45, 50, 58, 92, 102-4,
    Concertos]   117, 119, 120, 160, 161.
        No. 1 for piano   126, 127, 129
        No. 2 for piano   104, 125, 126, 129
        for violin   120, 126, 131, 132
        for violin and cello 126, 135
    Requiem   14, 160
    Symphonies
        No. 1 in C minor   39, 48, 102, 103
        No. 2 in D   71, 102, 103

Brahms, Johannes—*continued*.
    Symphonies
        No. 3 in F   48, 82, 83, 102, 103-4
        No. 4 in E minor   8, 62, 102, 103, 104, 157
British Broadcasting Corporation   5, 144
B.B.C. Orchestra   3, 5, 7, 8
Britten, Benjamin   71
Bruch, Max   126, 132
Bruckner, Anton   116
Busch, Adolf   162
Busch, Fritz   7, 162
Byrd, William   19, 141

Chappell & Co.   6, 11
Chopin, Frederic, Concertos   129
Clementi, Muzio   9
Coates, Albert   160
Colles, Dr. H. C.   110, 116
Colonne, Edouard   6
Concert spirituel   21, 97
Corelli, Arcangelo   17
    Concertos.   119
        Christmas Concerto   122
Covent Garden.   152, 160, 161, 162
Crystal Palace Concerts   9, 10-1.

Debussy, Claude   25, 159
    L'Après-midi d'un Faune   63
    String Quartet.   89, 90
Delius, Frederick   43, 156
    Concerto for piano   130
    Hassan   138
    Mass of Life   26, 72
    Paris.   142
    Songs of Farewell   33
Denner, J. C.   44
Diaghilev's Ballet   160
Dittersdorf, Karl   141
Dvorak, Antonin   43, 92, 109, 140
    Concerto for violoncello   133
    Symphonies
        No. 2.   108
        No. 4 in G   108
        No. 5 (*New World*)   108, 159
Dyson, Sir George   113
Elgar, Sir Edward   6, 7, 48, 76, 81, 110-1, 120,
               146, 147, 152, 159
    Cockaigne Overture   140
    Concertos
        for violin   120, 131, 132
        for violoncello   133
    Dream of Gerontius   63
    Enigma Variations   45, 59, 60
    Falstaff   143
    Introduction and Allegro   71, 123, 160
    Symphonies
        No. 1 in A flat   110
        No. 2 in E flat   62, 110-1, 157

Enesco, Georges   132
Equal Temperament   33
Erard, Sebastian   66
Esterhazy, Prince   94, 95

Falla, Manuel de   110
      Nights in the Gardens of Spain   127
      Tricorne.   139
Field, John.   161
Fisher, H. A. L.   13
Flecker, J. E.   138
Fogg, Eric.
      Concerto for bassoon   134
Formant.   34, 35
Forsyth, Cecil   49
Franck, César   43, 89, 90, 92, 111
      Djinns, Les.   127
      Symphony in D minor.   89
      Variations Symphoniques.   127
Furtwängler, Wilhelm   105, 151, 161-2

Gabrieli, Giovanni   121
Glazounov   109, 130
      Symphony No. 6   110
Gluck   15, 21, 24, 56
      Alceste   26
      Iphegenia in Tauris   39
      Orpheus   21, 26, 39
Glyndebourne Opera   7, 8, 162
Goethe   102, 138, 142
Goossens, Eugene   41, 162-3
Goossens, Léon   36, 41, 134
Gounod, Charles
      Faust   144
Gramophone   3, 108 (note), 116 and Appendix I
Grieg, Eduard   110
      Concerto for piano   130
      Peer Gynt   138
Grove, Sir George   10, 11
      Dictionary of Music and Musicians   11, 159

Hadow, W. H.   99
Hallé Orchestra   6, 152
Handel, George Frederick   18, 36, 40, 48, 93, 146, 151, 161
      Concertos   119
        for Organ   121, 122
        Twelve Grand Concertos   122
      Giulio Cesare   67
      Messiah   14, 54
      Saul   64
      Water Music   161
Harty, Sir Hamilton   8, 160-1
Haydn, Franz Joseph   3, 9, 13, 17, 18, 73, 80, 81,
                           87, 88, 91, 92, 94-6, 98, 100,
                           124, 141

Haydn, Franz Joseph—*continued*.
    Concertos   128
      for cello   133
      for trumpet   134
    Creation   95
    Symphonies   94-6
      Drum Roll   95
      Farewell   94
      London Symphonies   99
      In D, No. 7   95
      Military   61, 63
      Oxford   95
      Surprise   94
      Toy.   63
Heckel   43
Heifetz, Jascha   132
Helmholtz   34, 35
Henschel, Sir George   6
Hindemith, Paul   117
    Mathis the Painter   117, 144
Holst, Gustav   2, 64, 111
    Hymn of Jesus   79
    Planets   27, 57, 63, 64
    Psalm 148   79
Horsley, William   9

Indy, Vincent D'   116

Jacob, Gordon   41
Jazz   47, 54, 56, 58, 65, 70, 13
Joachim, Joseph   120

Kaulbach, Wilhelm von   142
Köchel catalogue   22
Kosleck   54
Koussevitsky, Sergei   152, 155
Kraft, Anton   133

Lambert, Constant   110
    Concerto for piano   131
    Rio Grande   64, 65, 161
Leeds Triennial Festival   3, 6, 54, 156
Liszt, Franz   89, 120, 142, 161
    Battle of the Huns   142
    Concertos for piano   63, 130
    Faust Symphony   15
    Tasso   142
London Philharmonic Orchestra   5, 7, 8, 10, 50, 156
London Symphony Orchestra   5, 6, 7, 8, 145

Maconchy, Elisabeth   134
Mackenzie, Sir Alexander   11
    Scottish Concerto   131
Mahler, Gustav   15, 58, 116
Mannheim   20, 21, 45, 93, 121
Manns, August   11
Massine, Leonide   107
McDougall, William   150

Mendelssohn, Felix   10, 24, 25, 100, 138, 140, 142
     Calm Sea and Prosperous Voyage 45, 59
     Concertos
         for piano   126
         for violin   126, 131
         Elijah   56,
         Hebrides Overture   106, 139, 156
         Hymn of Praise   15
         Italian Symphony   104, 106
         Ruy Blas Overture 139
         Scottish Symphony 104, 106
Mengelberg, Willem   5, 116, 152
Menuhin, Yehudi   132
Meyerbeer, Giacomo
         Le Prophète   26
         Les Huguenots   26, 46
Moeran, E. J.   113
Monteverde, Claudio   58, 67
         Orfeo   15, 139
Moussorgsky, Modeste
         Pictures at an Exhibition 147
Mozart, Wolfgang Amadeus   14, 15, 45, 56, 87, 92, 93,
                            94, 95, 96-9, 100, 105, 119, 133
     Orchestration   22-23, 37
     Cantata Freemasonry   72
     Concertos   124-5
         for bassoon (*K* 191)   48, 134
         for clarinet (*K* 662)   45, 134
         for flute (*K* 313-5)   134
         for horn (*K* 371, 412, 417, 447, 495, 514)   134
         for oboe (*K* 293)   41
         for piano
            in A (*K* 414)   128
            in A (*K* 488)   129
            in B flat (*K* 595)   129
            in C (*K* 503)   129
            in C minor (*K* 491)   125, 129
            in D (*K* 537)   129
         for violin   131-2
            in D (*K* 271a)   132
            in E flat (*K* 268)   132
            '*Adelaide*'   132
         for violin and viola (*K* 364)—*Sinfonia concertante* 124,
                              133, 135
     Divertimenti   23, 138
     Eine kleine Nachtmusik   71
     Operas :
         Clemenzia di Tito   26, 46
         Don Giovanni   99
         Entführung aus dem Serail see *Seraglio*
         Figaro   98, 139
         Seraglio   46, 63, 97
         Zauberflöte (**Magic Flute**) 46, 64
     Requiem Mass   26, 46, 56
     Symphonies
         in A (*K* 201)   96
         in C (*Jupiter K* 551)   82, 83 98, 99, 103

Mozart, Wolfgang Amadeus, Symphonies—*continued.*
   in E flat (*K* 543) 23, 98, 99
   in G minor (*K* 550) 23, 98, 99
   Haffner (*K* 385) 97
   Linz (*K* 425) 97, 98
   Paris (*K* 297) 21, 22-3, 97
   Prague (*K* 504) 22, 98
Mühlfeld, R 45
Musicians' Union 8
Mustel, V 64

Neate, Charles 9
Neel, Boyd 71
New Queen's Hall Orchestra 6
New York Philharmonic Symphony Orchestra 3
Newman, Robert 5, 6, 11
Newmarch, Mrs. Rosa 158
Nikisch, Artur 6, 153
Norwich Festival 3
Novello, Vincent 9

Orchestras
   Berlin Philharmonic 3, 4, 60, 161
   Boston Symphony 3
   Bournemouth Municipal 6, 8, 60
   B.B.C. 3, 5, 7, 8
   Hallé 6, 152
   London Philharmonic 5, 7, 8, 10, 50, 156
   London Symphony 5, 6, 7, 8, 145
   New Queen's Hall 6
   New York Philharmonic Symphony 3
   Philadelphia 162
   Queen's Hall 5-6
   Scottish 6
   Vienna Philharmonic 3
Overture
   Concert 139-40
   French 88, 93
   Italian 92, 93
Ovid 141

Paderewski, Ignaz 120
Paganini, Niccolo 120
Paget, Sir Richard 35
Palestrina 19, 73
Parry, Sir Hubert 11, 111
   Art of Music, (quoted) 75
Philadelphia Orchestra 162
Playford *The Dancing Master* 80
Plato 91
Priestley, J. B. 103
Prokofiev, Sergei 165
   Concerto for piano 131
   Concertos for violin 133
   Peter and the Wolf 116, 143
   Symphonie Classique 116
Promenade Concerts 5-6, 8, 11-12, 145, 152, 157
Puccini, Giacomo
   Madam Butterfly 63
   Gianni Schicchi 71

Purcell, Henry   17, 26, 58, 71, 80, 138, 146
   Chaconnes   71, 138
Quantz, J. J.   39
Queen's Hall   3, 6, 8, 11, 157, 160
Queen's Hall Orchestra   5, 6
Rachmaninov, Sergei   110, 120
      Bells   64
      Concertos for piano   126, 130
      Paganini Rhapsody   127, 130
Raff, J. J.   10
Randegger, Alberto   6
Ravel, Maurice   147
      Bolero   47, 64
      Concertos for piano   130-1
      Daphnis et Chloe   139, 157
Reed, W. H.   6, 120
Respighi, Ottorino   132, 142
Richter, F. Xavier   93
Richter, Hans   6, 110, 152
Rimsky-Korsakov, Nicholas   109
      Antar   110
      Scheherezade   56, 110
      Sinfonietta   109
Robertson, Rae   135
Ronald, Sir Landon   159
Rossini, G. A.   21
Roussel, Albert   116
Royal Academy of Music   157
Royal College of Music   11, 162
Royal Philharmonic Society   5, 9-10, 144
Rubinstein, Anton   10, 110, 130,
Saint-Saens, Camille   64
   Concertos   130, 131, 132, 133
Salomon, J. P.   3, 9, 17, 63, 95
Sargent, Dr. Malcolm   110, 153, 158-9
Sax, Adolph   46, 58
Scarlatti, Domenico   151
   Sonatas   80
Scherchen, Hermann   57, 150, 151
Schiller   101
Schnabel, Artur   158
Schubert, Franz   10, 81, 98, 104-105
      Rosamunde   11
   Symphonies
      No. 4 (Tragic)   105
      No. 5   105
      No. 7. C major   41, 105, 157
      No. 8. (Unfinished)   41, 89, 105
Schumann, Robert   24, 130, 149, 151
   Concertos
      for cello   133
      for piano   126, 129-30, 133
      for violin   132
   Symphonies
      Rhenish   104, 106
      Spring   106
Scottish Orchestra   6

Scriabin, Alexander   160
Shore, Bernard   134
        The Orchestra Speaks   151, 152, 155, 161
Shostakovitch, Dimitri   116, 161
Sibelius, Jean   110, 120, 158
        Concerto for violin   132
        En Saga   61
        Finlandia   142
    Symphonies   81, 88, 89, 92, 114-5, 156
        Tempest   138
Smetana, Bedrich   140, 142
Spohr, Ludwig   70, 142
Stadler, Maximilian   45, 134
Stamitz, Johann   18, 20, 45, 93
Stanford, Sir Charles V.   11, 111, 154-5
        Concerto for clarinet   45, 134
Steinbach, Fritz   6
Stokowski, Leopold   155, 162
Strauss, Johann
        Waltzes   138
Strauss, Richard   24, 43, 46, 115, 117
        Burlesca   127
        Don Juan   142
        Don Quixote   57, 71, 134, 141-2
        Heldenleben   26, 27, 41, 43, 143
        Macbeth   142
        Rosenkavalier   64
        Salome   26, 71
        Till Eulenspiegel   51, 63, 142, 151
        Tod und Verklärung   142
        Zarathustra   142
Stravinsky, Igor   12, 70, 151
        Noces   135
        Oiseau de Feu   138
        Petrouchka   138
        Sacre du Printemps   60, 63, 139
Sullivan, Sir Arthur   11, 158
Symphonic Poem   142-3

Tchaikovsky, Peter Ilich   29, 92, 99, 107-8, 110, 116, 120,
    Ballets]   147, 158
        Casse-noisette   46, 64, 138
        Lac des Cygnes   138
        Sleeping Princess   138
    Concertos   126, 130
        for piano in B flat minor   127
        for violin   120, 132
    Overture : 1812   61
    Rococo Variations   133
    Symphonies
        No. 4   29, 106, 107, 109
        No. 5   45, 51, 107
        No. 6   107, 108
    Symphonic Poems
        Francesca da Rimini   142
        Hamlet   142
        Romeo and Juliet   142

Tertis, Lionel   41, 134
Three Choirs Festival   3, 6
The Times   4
Toscanini, Arturo   3, 44, 151, 159-60
Tovey, Sir Donald   125, 133, 144
Transcriptions   146-7, 151
Transposing instruments   41-53

Uday Shankar   62

Valves   49-51
Vaughan Williams, Ralph   81, 88, 115
    Concertos
      for piano   131
      for violin (Accademico)   132
      Job   47, 139
    Symphonies
      in F minor   112
      London   111
      Pastoral   111
      Sea   111
    Wasps Overture   140
Verdi, Giuseppe   159
    Aida   26
    Requiem   14, 61, 160
    Rigoletto   71
Vienna Philharmonic Orchestra   3
Vieuxtemps, Henri   120
Viols   16-17, 67
Vivaldi, Antonio   127, 128

Wagner, Richard   15, 18, 24, 26, 27, 58, 73, 100,
                                            101, 140, 144, 145, 147, 152
    Lohengrin   139, 156
    Meistersinger   41, 62, 64, 139, 159, 162
    Parsifal   70
    The Ring   26, 45, 46, 57, 64, 141, 145, 154,
    Tannhäuser   139   [156, 162
    Tristan   43, 46, 145, 151
Wagner tubas   57
Walter, Bruno   151
Walton, William   147
    Symphony   88, 90, 113, 161
    Concerto for viola   125, 134
    Concerto for violin   132
Webbe, Samuel   9
Weber, Carl Maria von   140
    Concerto for bassoon   134
    Concerto for clarinet   45, 134
    Euryanthe   139
    Freischütz   40, 139
    Oberon   139
Weingartner, Felix   3, 105, 108, 151, 155, 161
Whittaker, Dr. W. G.   53
Wieniawski, Henri   120
Wood, Sir Henry J.   5, 6, 8, 11, 12, 114, 145, 147,
                                            152, 153, 155, 157-8